Accessing the General Curriculum

Accessing the General Curriculum

Including Students With Disabilities in Standards-Based Reform

Victor Nolet

Margaret J. McLaughlin

Foreword by Vincent Ferrandino
Executive Director, National Association of Elementary School Principals

CORWIN PRESS, INC.
A Sage Publications Company
Thousand Oaks, California

For information:

Corwin Press, Inc.
A Sage Publications Company
2455 Teller Road
Thousand Oaks, California 91320
E-mail: order@corwinpress.com

Sage Publications Ltd.
6 Bonhill Street
London EC2A 4PU
United Kingdom

Sage Publications India Pvt. Ltd.
M-32 Market
Greater Kailash I
New Delhi 110 048 India

Printed in the United States of America

Library of Congress Cataloging-in-Publication Data

Nolet, Victor.
    Accessing the general curriculum: Including students with disabilities in standards-based reform /
    by Victor Nolet and Margaret McLaughlin.
        p.   cm.
    Includes bibliographical references and index.
    ISBN 0-7619-7669-8—ISBN 0-7619-7670-1 (pbk.)
    1. Special education—United States—Curricula. 2. Handicapped
    children—Education—United States. 3. Inclusive education—United States.
I. McLaughlin,
Margaret J.
    II. Title.
    LC3981.N65 2000
    371.9′046—dc21   00-009023

This book is printed on acid-free paper.

02 03 04 05 10 9 8 7 6 5 4 3

Corwin Editorial Assistant: Kylee Liegl
Production Editor: Astrid Virding
Editorial Assistant: Candice Crosetti
Typesetter: D&G Limited, LLC

This is the first book I have seen on the topic.that is written at this level—it is needed and well done. Others have been much more theory laden with little practical information.

John Bruno, Assistant Professor
Dept. of Special Education
Florida State University

IDEA 97 made access to the general education curriculum a legal mandate. In Accessing the General Curriculum, *Nolet and McLaughlin have shown us the way to achieve it.*

Raymond W. Bryant, Director
Dept. of Special Education
Montgomery County Public Schools (MD)

This is a timely and well-conceived book based on principles and ideas that should be stan-dard issue for special educators, general educators, instructional leaders, and teacher prepa-ration professionals. With practical guides such as this one, general and special educators have anchors with which to hold onto as they begin exploring the most effective ways to make their curriculum accessible.

David J. Chard, Assistant Professor
Dept. of Special Education
University of Texas—Austin

Accessing the General Curriculum *masterfully outlines strategies for teachers and admin-istrators to utilize to strike a balance between the needs of the student with a disability and the needs of the regular education teacher, to be held accountable to course standards and expectations.*

Ann Clark, Principal
Vance High School (NC)
National Principal of the Year (1994)

I read the manuscript cover-to-cover twice—I'm looking forward to its publication!

Debi Gartland, Professor
Dept. of Reading, Special Education & Instructional Technology
Towson University

There are many of us who need this information now—*educators need to take a hard, close look at themselves and how we provide for children.*

Janie R. Hatton, Principal
Pulaski High School (WI)
1st National Principal of the Year (1993)

The 97 amendments to IDEA make it clear that students with disabilities must have access to the general education curriculum. Simply put, students with disabilities should be learning the same challenging curriculum as other students. Though this is a simple concept, the diverse needs of the students with disabilities make implementation of this requirement complex. As always, Nolet and McLaughlin have provided the field with a valuable resource for meeting this challenge.

Tom Hehir, Former Director
Office of Special Education Programs
U.S. Dept. of Education

The book offers ways that both the general and special educator can effectively work together to promote student achievement. The book takes what we know about best practices in special education and effectively weaves it to align with the general curriculum. Excellent solutions for accessing the general curriculum are provided, including aligning the curriculum with standards-based reform.

Asha Jitendra, Associate Professor
Dept. of Education & Human Services
Lehigh University

This book is excellent! I have not enjoyed such a good special education read in some time! The authors clearly and articulately spell out a plan for implementing the provisions of two major reform initiatives simultaneously; IDEA-97 and standards-based reform.

Anne Jordan, Professor
Dept. of Curriculum, Teaching & Learning
Ontario Institute for the Study of Education
University of Toronto

This is an excellent, easy-to-understand explanation of what can be confusing concepts for many preservice and inservice teachers.

Nancy Mamlin, Professor
Dept. of Language, Reading, & Exceptionalities
Appalachian State University

This is a book for all teachers, all administrators and I would encourage parents to read it. If they had this understanding, they would be much more effective in IEP meetings, in asking the right questions, and in actually assisting the staff in writing quality goals. It is an excellent piece of work, well documented with research and examples, and the readability of the manuscript is appropriate.

Marion Morehouse, Principal
Cascade Middle School (OR)
Oregon Principal of the Year (1997)

I have not seen a work that comes even close to presenting such crucial information as this in a clear manner. By keeping the suggestions grounded in practical and uncomplicated processes the authors ensure that any teacher can implement the suggested strategies in just about any circumstance.

Joseph Staub, Teacher
Thomas Starr King Middle School
Los Angeles Unified School District (CA)

REVIEWERS

Janie Hatton
Principal
Pulaski High School
Milwaukee, WI

Thomas Hehir
Former Director
Office of Special Education Programs
Graduate School of Education
Harvard University
Cambridge, MA

Asha Jitendra
Associate Professor
Dept. of Education & Human Services
Lehigh University
Bethlehem, PA

Anne Jordan
Professor
Dept. of Curriculum, Teaching & Learning
Ontario Institute for the Study of Education
University of Toronto
Toronto, Ontario

Mary Male
Professor
Dept. of Special Education & Rehab. Services
San Jose State University
San Jose, CA

Nancy Mamlin
Professor
Dept. of Language, Reading, & Exceptionalities
Appalachian State University
Boone, NC

Marion Morehouse
Principal
Cascade Middle School
Bend, OR

Trinka Messenheimer
Assistant Professor
School of Education & Intervention Services
Bowling Green State University
Bowling Green, OH

Joseph Staub
Teacher
Thomas Starr King Middle School
Los Angeles Unified School District
Los Angeles, CA

CONTENTS

ACKNOWLEDGEMENTS

The authors would like to thank the following people for their invaluable assistance in the preparation of this book: Valerie Foster and Elizabeth Caron at the University of Maryland and Pamela Hamilton at Western Washington University. Thanks also to Asha Jitendra at Leigh University and Terresa Gibney at Western Washington University for their extremely helpful feedback on early drafts of Chapters 3 and 4. Finally, thank you to Robb Clouse at Corwin Press for his unflagging support and enthusiasm for this project.

FOREWORD

Making Schools Work for Students with Disabilities

There is probably no other issue that will engender such strong emotions for teachers and administrators than the challenge of making the school's general curriculum accessible for students with disabilities. For too long, "regular" educators and "special" educators have been embroiled in an us-them debate as to whose responsibility it is to provide instructional services for students with disabilities.

This book will go a long way to put that debate to rest. The authors provide a highly useful and rational approach to addressing this challenge. Both have had extensive theoretical and practical experience working with students and educators in real schools. They bring a deep and clear understanding of what the Individuals with Disabilities Education Act of 1997 (IDEA-97) legislation requires and how it can be implemented in real-life situations in our nation's schools. They do so from the framework of providing for the needs of *all* the children in the classroom. Although they come from a special education background, they have a firm grasp of the realities of today's classrooms. Their recommendations are well grounded and highly implemented.

The authors are careful to link their discussion of IDEA-97 with a solid understanding of curriculum and the standards-based reforms that are now a permanent part of the educational landscape across the nation. Teachers, principals, and other administrators would do well to use the first few chapters of this book as a comprehensive review of the latest version of IDEA, the nature of curriculum in our schools, and the teaching-learning process. The aspiring educator will find these chapters to be a concise and clear description of these issues that are often difficult to understand.

Most significantly, perhaps, this book dispels the traditional model of special education where students with disabilities were viewed in isolation from general education. In its place, the authors offer an outline of a new model in which a set of services and support provides students with access to the general education curriculum. In this model, decisions about an Innovative Educational Program (IEP) are still individualized, but they start from the expectations of the general curriculum and what is required to help the student access that curriculum.

With this as the premise, readers are taken through a comprehensive, easy-to-understand discussion on how to implement this new model. The illustrations are taken from situations that will be very familiar to educators. It becomes quickly evident that this new model enables all educators, "special" and "regular," to address the challenges of making the curriculum accessible for students with disabilities in a more rational and effective manner.

This book makes a substantial contribution to a critical area of education. It is a balanced work, taking into consideration the requirements of IDEA-97 and the realities of today's schools. More than a "how-to" book, this work provides educators with a new way to look at one of the most challenging issues before us. It will serve as a valuable resource for everyone interested in providing students with an education that meets both the letter and the spirit of IDEA-97.

Vincent L. Ferrandino
Executive Director
National Association of Elementary School Principals

INTRODUCTION

One of the bedrock principles of special education is that all students who have disabilities have the right to a free appropriate public education. This assumption is based largely on the equal protection provisions of the Fourteenth Amendment to the U.S. Constitution. The outcomes associated with public schooling are so highly valued in our culture, that the courts view denial of access to a public education as being tantamount to the denial of life, liberty, or property.

When it has been applied in schools, the idea of *equal protection* generally has been interpreted as *equal access*—usually access to a place such as a particular school building or classroom. The 1975 special education legislation went further than merely guaranteeing access to "public education." It also entitled a student with disabilities to an "appropriate" education. However, what was considered appropriate was left to the team that developed the individual education program for each child.

The focus on individually designed education is the hallmark of special education. Yet the relation of the individualized education plan to general education classroom practices never was explicitly defined until the Individuals with Disabilities Education Act was reauthorized in 1997 (P.L. 105-17, commonly known as IDEA-97). The law now includes language that, for the first time, clearly communicates the expectation that *access* involves something more than merely the location at which special education is delivered. Although still referenced to the individual, special education now must be connected to the general education curriculum. In fact, IDEA-97 asserts that the education of students who have disabilities can be made more effective when schools ensure their *access in the general curriculum to the maximum extent possible* [Sec. 601 (c)(5)].

The law now clearly emphasizes the principle that the education of all children should be anchored in the general education curriculum. The implications are potentially huge for everyone in public schools who works with students who have disabilities, but particularly for teachers and administrators. The purpose of this book is to help teachers and school administrators begin to translate policy into practice as we explore the meaning and implications of "access to the general curriculum."

ACCESSING THE GENERAL CURRICULUM

New IDEA Requirements and What They Mean

The 1997 amendments to the Individuals with Disabilities Education Act (P.L. 105-17) represent a major advancement in ensuring that each student with a disability receives a high quality and individually designed education. The amendments build on the original purposes of law: each student must be ensured a free appropriate public education, each child's education must be determined on an individualized basis and designed to meet his or her particular needs in the least restrictive environment, and the rights of children and their families must be ensured and protected through procedural safeguards. In addition, a system of support programs must be available to ensure that schools hire well-qualified teachers, that new knowledge about how best to educate students with disabilities is translated into school programs, and that a broad system of technical assistance will exist to help states and local school districts implement special education and related services. The IDEA-97 amendments retain these basic civil rights protections and educational provisions but also include some important changes that we will explore here.

Why Has IDEA Changed?

There is no question that IDEA has had a positive impact on the lives of students with disabilities. Significant progress has been made to create educational opportunities for all of our nation's children and youth with disabilities that were unavailable 20, or even 10, years ago. Today every eligible student with a disability is guaranteed access to a free public education. Over five million such students are now being educated in the U.S. schools and the majority of these students are receiving more than half of their education in general education classrooms. So why change something that has had such a positive impact?

Although great progress has been made, significant challenges remain. Despite decades of participation in public education, achievement outcomes for students with disabilities are still less than what we know we can accomplish. Too many of these students are failing courses and dropping out of school because they don't have appropriate interventions or supplementary aids and services. Enrollment of students with disabilities in post-secondary education is still too low and, while employment rates are improving, they still are unsatisfactory for students with learning problems. It is these challenges that have prompted changes in IDEA.

The 1997 reauthorization is intended to ensure that students with disabilities have access to challenging curriculum and that their educational programs are based on high expectations that acknowledge each student's potential and ultimate contribution to society. To do this, the new IDEA provisions have begun to shift the focus of education from physical access toward educational performance. Specifically, IDEA-97 is intended to better align special education programs and policies with the larger national school improvement effort referred to as *standards-based reform*.

What Is Standards-Based Reform?

Standards-based reform is a policy response to the dissatisfaction with the performance of American schools that has been growing in both the public and private sectors for a number of years. Major elements of standards-based reform are (a) higher content standards, (b) the use of assessments aimed at measuring how schools are helping students meet the standards, and (c) an emphasis on holding educators and students accountable for student achievement.

Standards

The core of the reforms rests on *standards*. Standards are general statements of what students should know or be able to do as a result of a pub-

Box 1.1   Pubic Opinions About School Reform

Public dissatisfaction with schools has fueled the standards-based reform movement. Consider these findings from recent opinion polls:

- Seventy-one percent of Americans surveyed supported a voluntary national testing program that would routinely test fourth- and eighth-grade students in order to measure the performance of the nation's public schools (Rose and Gallup, 1998).

- Eighty-three percent of Americans surveyed said that standards would help improve student academic performance (Public Agenda, 1998).

- Eighty-one percent of parents surveyed favored requiring students to meet certain basic standards before they can pass to the next grade level (Public Agenda, Febrary 1977).

lic school education. During the last decade, standards were incorporated into school reform legislation passed in most states.

No "standard" exists for these new state standards. State and local district standards differ on many dimensions. Some only apply to specific subjects such as math, science, language arts, writing, or social studies. Other standards address areas such as physical well being or technology. Some standards are broad statements of learner goals ("becoming self sufficient learners"), while others are very specific about what students should be able to know and do in math or science at specific grade or age levels. Most standards require an "authentic" application of knowledge in solving real-life problems or creating real-life tasks.

Assessment

New assessments and accountability requirements are being implemented nationwide. Many of these programs use a variety of innovative assessment procedures such as performance tasks, portfolios, and extended constructed responses in addition to traditional multiple-choice tests. The premise of the new assessments is that students should be asked to demonstrate the skilled use of knowledge to solve complex problems rather than to reiterate rote-memorized facts. These assessments may range from something as basic as writing in response to a simple prompt to elaborate projects or performances evaluated as part of a portfolio.

Accountability

An increased demand for accountability has changed the consequences for schools and individual students. School-level accountability usually is achieved through school reports that summarize student test results and other student data such as attendance and graduation rates.

In some places, student assessment results are used in new accreditation or school inspection systems. Some states have also attached rewards, such as grants or cash incentives, and/or sanctions such as school takeovers due to student achievement results. At the student level, accountability may mean that test scores are linked to promotions from grade to grade or to high school graduation. Throughout all standards-based reforms, there is an overriding emphasis on higher levels of student achievement and the stakes are high for schools, teachers, and students.

How Does IDEA-97 Align with Standards-Based Reform?

The new requirements in the 1997 amendments are aligned with the components of standards-based reform. These include changes in Innovative Educational Programs (IEP) requirements as well as several new provisions relating to assessment and accountability.

New IEP Provisions

Several changes to the IEP requirements require specific attention to how an individual student will access the general education curriculum *regardless of the setting in which she/he will receive special education and related services*. The IEP must now include the following:

* A statement of the child's present levels of educational performance, *including how the child's disability affects their involvement and progress in the general curriculum*. For preschool children, there must be a statement of how the disability affects the child's participation in appropriate activities.

* Measurable annual goals, including benchmarks or short-term objectives, related to meeting the child's needs that result from her or his disability. These goals and objectives must enable the child to be involved in and *progress in the general curriculum* while at the same time meeting each of the child's other unique educational needs.

* A statement of the special education and related services, supplementary aids and services, or program modifications that are to be provided to the child. Also, there must be a description of any modifications or supports for school personnel that are necessary for the child to advance toward attaining the annual goals, *be involved and progress in the general curriculum*, participate in extracurricular or other nonacademic activities, and to

be educated and participate in activities with other children with and without disabilities.

- An explanation of the extent, if any, to which the child will *not* participate with the children without disabilities in general education classes and activities.

- A statement of any individual modifications in the administration of state or district assessments of student achievement that are needed for the child to participate in the assessment. If the IEP team determines that the child will not participate in the assessment, the IEP must include a statement that tells why that assessment is not appropriate along with a description of how the child's achievement will be measured.

- A statement of how the child's progress toward the annual goals will be measured and how the child's parents will be regularly informed of that progress. This notification also must include an assessment of whether the student's progress is sufficient to enable him or her to achieve the goals by the end of the year.

Participation in Assessments

The 1997 IDEA legislation requires that children with disabilities be included in general education state and district assessment programs, with accommodations as needed. Exceptions can be made only if participation will invalidate the assessments or if reporting will result in disclosure of the identity of individual students with disabilities. For students with disabilities who cannot participate in state and district assessments, the states and local districts must develop guidelines for their participation in alternate assessments and report the performance of these students along with that of their non-disabled peers. Although the federal law does not prescribe the proportion of students who might take an alternative assessment, the expectation is that the vast majority of students with disabilities will take the general assessments.

Performance Goals and Indicators

States are required to establish goals for the performance of children and youth with disabilities and to develop indicators to judge the progress of students on these goals. States previously were required only to provide data on students with disabilities in several areas, such as numbers of students served by age and disability, the settings in which services are provided, and certain exit outcomes. However, this new provision requires states to examine critical indicators of student progress. Both traditional student assessment data and other outcomes considered important for students with disabilities must now be examined.

School-based Improvement Plans

States now are allowed to grant authority to local districts to select individual schools to design and implement a schoolwide improvement plan for students with disabilities as well as other students. These plans are intended to include the full participation of all members of that school community and be grounded in schoolwide goals and indicators. Moreover, the plans must include sound assessment procedures that will show how well students with disabilities are meeting those schoolwide goals.

The Link Between "Standards" and Curriculum

As special educators approach the challenge of providing access to new and challenging material, it is important that they understand the link between standards, the general education curriculum, and a student's IEP. Essentially, two types of standards exist: *content* standards and *performance* standards. Content standards refer to what gets taught, the subject matter, the skills and knowledge, and the applications. Performance standards set the targets or levels of "mastery" that students must meet in various subject matter. Content standards reflect what professional educators and the community at large believe that schools should teach. The content standards set the broad curriculum goals. Performance standards translate that content into specific knowledge and skills that students are expected to demonstrate. Such standards usually are defined at specific grade levels or benchmark years. In other words, performance standards really set the targets for teachers. They specify that "by the time they reach this particular grade, we expect students to be able to do these specific things and know this specific information."

Together content and performance standards are intended to be a guide for redesigning the general education curriculum. Standards are very important because they determine *what* teachers are expected to teach at specific grade levels. Increasingly, they also are defining *how* teachers should teach the content. Standards as a guide for curriculum are less than perfect. First, tremendous variability takes place across states and local school districts in terms of how specifically the standards are stated. Some standards focus on global goals such as, "Modify or affirm scientific ideas according to accumulated evidence." Others are more precise statements of specific skills expected to be mastered at certain grade levels such as, "Identify and explain major issues, movements, people, and events in U.S. history from its beginnings to 1877 with particular emphasis on change and continuity, such as the American Revolution, the emergence of sectional differences, and the Civil War."

The primary purposes of the content and performance standards are to (a) focus the general education curriculum on a core of important and challenging content, and (b) ensure that *every* student in a state or district receives instruction in the *same* challenging content.

Current Issues with Standards and Curriculum

A number of issues surround standards-based reforms. First is the issue that most standards have been defined through a group consensus process, using input from educators with expertise in specific subject matter, actual professionals in specific fields such as scientists or business persons, and community members. As a result, defining what schools should teach has been a political process in some places, sometimes resulting in great controversy. Also, most of the content standards that have been developed to date refer almost exclusively to the traditional academic content areas of reading/language arts, math, science, and social science/history/civics (McDonnell, McLaughlin, Morrison, 1997; Gandal, 1996). So far, even when a state or district develops standards in areas such as career or vocational skills, physical well being, or the arts, only the academic areas are assessed.

Indeed, discussions about what public schools should teach occurred frequently during the 20th century as public sentiment changed. Scholars and researchers often had differences of opinion about what constituted good teaching, and state and local policies often reflected public or political demands to increase student achievement in different areas.

For example, the 1920s and 1930s saw a diversification of curriculum, including more emphasis on "manual" or work skills. This change was in response to a greatly diversified student body as well as to the Great Depression. During the 1940s and 1950s, the emphasis on military superiority created emphasis on math and science education and the need to establish technological superiority in the United States. During the 1960s and 1970s, there was a heightened awareness of the need for curriculum and textbooks to portray the contributions of women and members of minority groups and to present the country's history in a more critical light (Manzo, 1998).

During the past two decades, the emphasis has shifted to global competition and the need to insure that all students, rich and poor, receive the same challenging content to prepare them for jobs in an information society. This most recent shift in public priority has resulted in an almost exclusively academic focus in content standards. When these academically focused standards are linked to assessments that are in turn tied to high school diplomas or other high stakes consequences for schools, it means that the general education curriculum is primarily pre-collegiate as opposed to vocational or technical. This poses problems for students with disabilities who often require extensive education in the career/vocational areas, particularly at middle and high school levels (McDonnell, et al., 1997; Rusch, 1992).

Another issue is the scope and intellectual challenge imposed by the new standards and curricula. Recent research conducted by Schmidt, McKnight, and Raizen (1997) compared science and math curricula around the world. These researchers analyzed textbooks and curriculum guides from the countries that participated in the Third International Mathematics and Science Study (TIMSS). They found that in the U.S., math and science curricula cover more topics by ninth grade than 50 to 75 percent of other countries and that new topics (skills, concepts, and so on) are added each year. In contrast, most other countries teach fewer concepts or topics each year, and they teach the content to mastery.

This "piling on" of content was a key finding in research conducted by McLaughlin and her colleagues (McLaughlin, Henderson, and Rhim, 1997; McLaughlin, Nolet, Rhim, and Henderson, 1999) in school districts across the country that were engaging in standards-based reform. Teachers in that study reported having more and more content to cover every semester. As a result, teachers felt that the pace of instruction had increased and they had little time to reteach or support students who required more demonstration or practice.

Complicating the number of topics that must be taught is the more complex nature of curriculum. Perhaps the two most influential standards documents are the National Council of Teachers of Mathematics (1989) mathematics standards and the National Academy of Science Standards. These documents have been widely adopted across the U.S. and form the basis for many of the statewide curriculum frameworks. The NCTM and National Academy standards set forth what is considered by these learned societies to be the critical content that all students are supposed to learn in math and science. The NCTM and National Academy standards emphasize strategic content and processes in place of rote memorization of facts or splinter skills. This approach to math and science teaching already is being translated into classroom practice as well as curriculum materials.

An examination of state math and science standards conducted by Blank and Pechman (1995) found an emphasis on applied problem solving and "authentic" knowledge. This approach required more active roles for students, less teacher-directed instruction, less rote skill development, and more emphasis on students' understanding of topics and how to link math and science than simply learning content.

The math and science standards reflect new theories and research about how children and adults learn. This research has shifted the focus from drill and practice to student understanding and the application of knowledge. The new content standards are changing the demands of the general education curriculum in some subject matter areas in at least two ways: increasing the amount of content and increasing the demands on the learner to engage in more complex applications and problem-solving.

Standards, Curriculum, and Students with Disabilities

For many special educators, the emphasis on access to the general education curriculum is more rhetorical than practical. They ask how a student in special education who has not already succeeded in some or all of the general curriculum can be expected to be instructed in that same material. In fact, the case study research involving high-reform local school districts (McLaughlin et al., 1999; McLaughlin et al., 1999) reveals that many general education teachers and administrators also are asking similar questions about what it means to provide access to the general education curriculum as well as why they should *want* to do this.

According to the most recent Annual Report to Congress, in 1994 and 1995 the majority of the 2.2 million American students between the ages 6 and 21 who have disabilities spent at least 80 percent of their school day in general education classes (U.S. Department of Education, 1997). Yet we know little about how these students are accessing the general education curriculum. Our knowledge is limited in this area in large part because students with disabilities have not been systematically included in large-scale national educational studies. What we do know is that secondary students with disabilities take fewer academic courses and more vocational courses than their non-disabled peers and have higher course failure rates and slightly lower grades than their peers (McDonnell et al., 1997; McGrew, Thurlow, and Spiegel, 1993; National Center for Educational Statistics, 1996; Rossi, 1997; Wagner, 1993).

A number of small research studies have documented the experiences of students with disabilities in general education classes. Specifically, these studies have examined efforts on the part of general educators to accommodate the needs of students with disabilities in their classrooms (McGregor and Vogelsberg, 1998; Klinger and Vaughn, 1999). The major conclusions drawn from these studies are that access to the general education curriculum means more than simply being present in a general education classroom. Access requires that students with disabilities be provided with the supports necessary to allow them to benefit from instruction. This requirement applies across all instructional domains. A student's IEP becomes the vehicle for determining how a student is to access the general education curriculum.

A New Way to Think About Special Education

The foundation of special education rests on the guarantee that each eligible student receive a "free and appropriate public education." What constitutes appropriate is to be determined on a student-by-student basis by parents and a multi-disciplinary team of professionals. These decisions become a student's IEP. The demand to link the IEP to the general education curriculum, which in turn links to standards, creates a new way of thinking about special education. The "traditional" model of special education viewed students with disabilities in isolation of general education. That is, a child was tested, his/her learning strengths and deficits identified, and individual goals, objectives, and strategies were devised to meet the deficits. However, the assessments frequently were conducted in isolation from the larger general education curriculum. The assessments focused on immediate and discrete skill deficits and IEPs often were a collection of isolated skill objectives that led to isolated instruction. The student's program may have been individualized, but it could also be separated from the larger scope and sequence of a curriculum. Too often, the IEP *became* the curriculum for the student, instead of a tool for defining how to implement a general education curriculum.

The "new" model of special education, illustrated in Figure 1.1, is one in which a set of services and supports provides a student access to the general education curriculum.

A student's IEP is based on an assessment that indicates what accommodations and/or modifications should be provided to help the student access the curriculum as well as the instructional strategies that will be required and how progress will be monitored. In addition, special education can supplement the general education curriculum by providing instruction in specific curricular areas or skill areas not addressed in the general education curriculum, such as in the social and behavioral areas or other more functional daily living skills. Decisions about an IEP are individualized, but they start from the expectations of the general education curriculum and what is required to help the student access that curriculum.

Challenges for Special Education Teachers

A number of challenges face special education teachers as they implement new reforms, such as standards and assessments with students with disabilities. The most significant of these challenges is to figure out what it means to enable a student to access the general education curriculum. If students do not have meaningful access to the general education curriculum, they cannot be expected to do well on state and local assessments. Poor performance in these assessments can lead to consequences for schools and students who may not be promoted from one grade to another or receive a high school diploma.

Therefore, *access to the general education curriculum* must mean providing an opportunity to learn the important content reflected in rigorous content standards. Access to the general education curriculum is the cornerstone of a student's IEP and therefore defines what will constitute special education and related services. Providing access will require much more of special education teachers than mastering certain assessment techniques or instructional practices. It will require that teachers truly understand what the curriculum is and how it relates to instruction.

Domains of Knowledge for Ensuring Access

The challenges general and special education teachers will face as they begin to interpret and implement the requirement of providing access to the general education curriculum will be difficult. The quick fixes and simplistic approaches have already been tried and rejected. Providing access to the general education curriculum will require a new way of thinking about special education and of students with disabilities. Instead of focusing on identifying student needs and deficits and designing interventions to address the deficits, we must begin with an expectation that each student will succeed in the general education curriculum and that every teacher has a role in providing instruction that meets the curricular goals. Teaching that ensures that all students have access to the general curriculum involves three domains: content knowledge, the processes involved in learning, and strategies for designing instruction.

Content knowledge is the "what" of access. It is the information contained in the curriculum and the essence of school learning. All other things being equal, teachers who have a more complete understanding of their content domain will be more able to design instruction that ensures access than teachers whose understanding of the content is fragile or superficial.

Teachers must fully understand the process that affects student learning and be able to plan instruction that matches those *learning processes*. Our understanding of how children learn has grown immensely in the last two decades and the instructional implications of recent research into human learning are profound.

Instructional design and adaptation is a systematic process of creating effective, universally accessible learning opportunities. All other things being equal, teachers who engage in a systematic design process to plan, implement, and evaluate instruction will be more likely to meet the needs of all students than those teachers who lack this critical pedagogical skill. Also, teachers who understand how instruction relates to the content of the curriculum and to student-learning processes will be better able to develop appropriate accommodations and modifications when needed.

These domains are not independent. For example, experts in a domain learn and use content information differently than novices. Humans engage different learning processes to learn different kinds of information, and different instructional strategies are required for different kinds of information and at different phases of the learning process. Teaching that ensures access to the general curriculum requires an integrated understanding of the separate and combined effects of all three of these domains in the teaching and learning process.

This book is designed to help you integrate these three domains of knowledge to ensure that all students have meaningful access to the general curriculum. In Chapter One, we discuss standards-based reform and the links between standards and curriculum. We also introduce the three Domains of Knowledge for Ensuring Access—Content Knowledge, Learning Processes, and Instructional Design and Adaptation. In Chapter 2, "Understanding What Curriculum Is," you will learn about curriculum. We will examine what the general education curriculum really is and how it influences what happens day to day in a classroom. In Chapter 3, "The Learning-Teaching Connection," we will discuss the recent research on human learning and the implications of this research for designing effective instruction. New ideas about learning underlie much of the school reform movement and are beginning to have a profound effect on every aspect of schooling. We will discuss the teaching implications of this research and provide you with a rationale for making instructional design decisions that match student learning. In Chapter 4, "Evaluating the Outcome of Access," we discuss assessment strategies to help you know when a student is succeeding in the general curriculum as well as how to monitor their progress. In Chapter 5, "Accessing the Curriculum and the Individual Education Program," we will provide strategies for developing an IEP that provides access to the general education curriculum. We also will talk about how to plan instruction that is accessible for all students as well as how to think about accommodations and modifications that might be necessary for students who have learning problems. In Chapter 6, "Creating the Conditions for Access," we discuss the contexts that must be created to support access and will illustrate how teachers apply these principles and strategies in classrooms in four distinctly different school districts. Finally, in the Appendix, we have provided a list of resources for teachers and administrators seeking additional information about some of the issues we discuss in the book.

As you will see, the challenge of making the general curriculum accessible for all students requires a new way of thinking and problem solving. Therefore, this is not a "how-to" book. It is a "how-to-think" book. We hope that it will stimulate conversations and actions in your own school that enable you to find new ways to be effective with all of your students.

Figure 1.1   Special education and the general curriculum

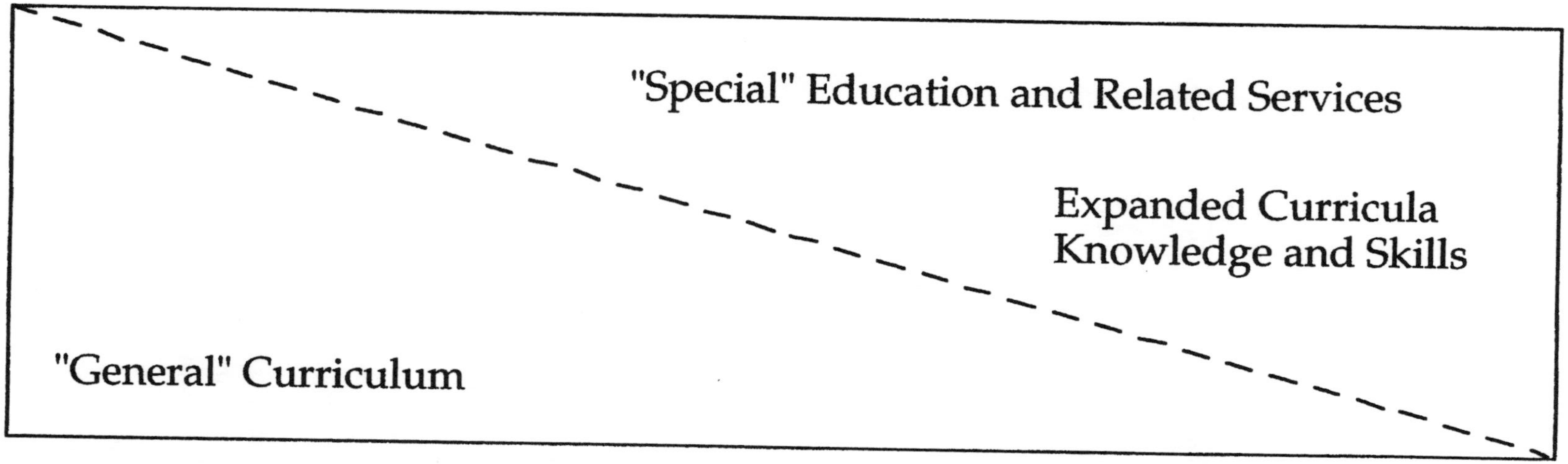

"Special" Education and Related Services

Expanded Curricula
Knowledge and Skills

"General" Curriculum

No Accommodations or Modifications	Accommodations	Modifications	Alternate
No changes to: • content • performance expectations • sequence and timelines • instruction	*No changes to:* • content • performance expectations *Changes to:* • sequence and timelines • instruction	*Changes some or all of:* • content areas • performance expectations • sequence and timelines • instruction	• individualized curriculum goals • separate functional curriculum

UNDERSTANDING WHAT CURRICULUM IS

Curriculum is at the center of standards-based reform, yet surprisingly little agreement exists among educators about the exact meaning of *curriculum*. For example, over 1,100 curriculum books were written during the 20th century and each offered its own variation on the meaning of the term (Cuban, 1992). Traditionally, curriculum has referred to any educational program lasting for several years, such as the courses taught in college and university programs or public schools. Public school practitioners often narrow the meaning of curriculum to refer almost exclusively to materials used in the classroom, primarily textbooks. Meanwhile, curriculum theorists often use the term more broadly to refer to the full range of experiences that students undertake under the guidance of schools. All of these interpretations of curriculum can be found in schools today and sometimes the precise interpretation of the term can only be derived from the context in which it is used.

In this chapter, we will examine the characteristics of public school K-12 curriculum, with particular attention to the general curriculum. As you will see, curriculum is complex and multifaceted. We believe that to truly understand what it means to "access" the general curriculum, you need to understand how curriculum works.

Multiple Types of Curriculum

The first thing to understand about curriculum is that it can have different meanings, depending on the perspective from which it is viewed. Often, these different meanings are referred to as *types* of curriculum. The three types of curriculum most pertinent to our discussion here are the *intended* curriculum, the *taught* curriculum, and the *learned* curriculum (Cuban, 1992).

The Intended Curriculum

The *intended curriculum* is the official or adopted curriculum often contained in state or district policy. This is the body of content that students are *expected* to learn as a result of their school experiences. Intended curricula generally take the form of formal, written documents that reflect the educational theory and societal values that prevail at a given time. The various curriculum frameworks currently in use in much of the United States are prime examples of intended curricula. Most state curriculum frameworks include broad descriptions of content domains and they often specify performance standards students would be expected to meet. There can be little doubt that the policy makers who formulate these guidelines and, by extension, the public these individuals represent *intend* that these curriculum frameworks will be the basis of instruction delivered in local schools. Indeed, many state and district assessments and school accountability measures are linked directly to the content and performance standards contained in the intended curriculum.

In addition to the curriculum frameworks associated with content and performance standards, state departments of education routinely issue guidelines specifying what subjects and skills are to be taught at each grade level. This has been particularly true at middle- and high-school levels where the intended curriculum often takes the form of graduation requirements.

The intended curriculum doesn't necessarily have to follow from government policy. Sometimes standards set by professional or certifying organizations constitute an intended curriculum. For example, schools offering an International Baccalaureate High School diploma follow a somewhat highly prescribed curriculum (Laurent-Brennan, 1998). Intended curricula developed at the local level may be somewhat narrowly defined, often pertaining to a specific subject area such as reading or writing. Teachers in a particular elementary school may decide among themselves what language arts skills they will teach at each grade level, or a district curriculum committee may develop a set of curriculum guidelines specifying how various aspects of social studies will be taught at each grade.

Although the Individualized Education Plan (IEP) developed for a particular student in special education specifies the goals and objectives a student is expected to meet, the IEP is *not* an intended curriculum for that student. Rather, the IEP is a plan for making the intended curriculum more immediate and specific for the student. The goals and objectives on a student's IEP should supplement and support the intended curriculum but not replace it.

The Taught Curriculum

The *taught curriculum* is the operationalization of the intended curriculum. The taught curriculum involves the minute-to-minute, day-to-day, and week-to-week events that actually occur in the classroom or other instructional settings. However, the taught curriculum is more than just lessons and activities. It includes teacher instructional behaviors, such as questioning or lecturing, and other instructional variables, such as time allocated for instruction, grouping arrangements, classroom rules, and materials. The taught curriculum also includes less formal aspects of teaching, such as incidental comments or conversations as well as the teacher beliefs and attitudes as they pertain to the intended curriculum. Sometimes these informal, unplanned events are what are most salient for students, as the situation in Box 2.1 illustrates.

The taught curriculum also includes curriculum materials such as textbooks, worksheets, and electronic media with which students interact. Although many teachers refer to curriculum materials such as textbooks as "the curriculum," this is a misnomer. Materials, no matter how well organized or how detailed, do not constitute a curriculum. Curriculum materials *do* exert a strong influence on the instruction that takes

Box 2.1   Mr. Painter Teaches About the Nile

Sometimes the taught curriculum has unintended side effects.

Mr. Painter's middle school class was engaged in a world geography lesson about Egypt. Instruction consisted of students takings turns reading aloud from their textbook round-robin style. While one student read aloud, the rest of the students followed along in their own books. Every once in a while, Mr. Painter would comment on the reading to help make the activity more interesting for the students. Following a passage that presented the fact "the longest river in Egypt is the Nile," the teacher made the following comment:

"Thank you, Mandy. Class, if you ever go to Egypt, don't stick your hand in the Nile because they have a little snail that lives there that can get into your skin and make you very sick. The disease you can get is called schistosomiasis. Schistosomiasis is a bad disease. You don't want to get it. Okay, Phillip, it's your turn to read."

Phillip then read the next paragraph in the text. The students in the class continued studying Egypt for the next three days. During that time, they read about the pyramids and mummies, looked at maps, completed a set of worksheets about the climate of North Africa, and watched a documentary about the Suez Canal. At no time during those three days was schistosomiasis ever mentioned or even alluded to again. On the fourth day after the Nile River lesson, the students were asked to write a brief essay about the most important things they had learned about Egypt and North Africa.

Out of 25 students in the class, 22 mentioned schistosomiasis or made some reference to a snail that lives in the Nile and causes illness. A total of eight students *only* discussed schistosomiasis in their essays, to the exclusion of all other topics addressed during the week. Only two of the students mentioned pyramids and none mentioned the Suez Canal. The students had been exposed to nearly five hours of instruction about Egypt, distributed over four days, yet the thing they most often remembered and to which they attached importance was a passing ten second comment from the teacher.

place in classrooms, but a teacher's use of curriculum materials varies considerably (Stodolsky, 1989). Curriculum materials, particularly textbooks, seem to affect teachers' choices of topics in areas such as reading (Barr and Dreeben, 1983) and math (Freeman and Porter, 1989), but textbooks are not a proxy for the taught curriculum. Teachers exercise wide latitude in variables such as how topics get covered, how much time is allocated to a topic, the kinds of activities and lessons that get used, and how students will be asked to use the information taught.

For many children, the IEP becomes the taught curriculum. That is, their entire educational program or program within a specific subject matter area is comprised of the specific goals and objectives contained in their IEP (Pugach and Warger, 1995). This has the same effect as textbooks, which is a drastic narrowing of the curriculum for these individuals. When the IEP is the taught curriculum, goals tend to be shortsighted and fragmented with little linkage to larger or longer-term outcomes.

The Learned Curriculum

The *learned curriculum* is what students actually learn as a result of being in the classroom and interacting with the intended and taught curricula. The learned curriculum includes the skills and knowledge that generally are associated with school learning as well as a wide variety of other information that may or may not be part of the intended or taught curricula. For example, a negative attitude about math may be learned from a teacher who models such an attitude, or students who experience repeated school failure may learn "helplessness."

The problem for teachers is that what their students learn may not be what they taught or what they intended them to learn. Most of the time, most students learn most of what their teachers expect them to learn. However, for some, the learned curriculum may include inaccuracies, misconceptions, and incomplete information. The only way we can ever know what it is students really have learned is to ask them to demonstrate it. Unfortunately, our inferences about what students learn are only as accurate as our assessment procedures, and many classroom testing procedures provide very poor information about the learned curriculum. One of the aims of alternative assessments, such as performance assessments and portfolios is to create more contextually relevant situations in which students can fully demonstrate what they have learned.

The Core Elements of Curriculum

As you can see, it is important to be clear about the type of curriculum (intended, taught, or learned) to which you are referring. Different aspects of curriculum may appear to be more or less dominant, depending on the context you are considering. However, three interrelated aspects of curriculum cut across all of the three types we discussed. These aspects underlie most of the decisions you will make about curriculum:

1. **Curriculum has a purpose.** Curriculum is planned and is linked to desired outcomes. These outcomes may be broadly defined (e.g., to prepare effective citizens) or they may be very specific (e.g., to teach children in the third grade to write in cursive).

2. **Curriculum involves a domain.** A domain is an identifiable body of information related to a particular knowledge or skill area. Specification of the domain defines the limits of what is and is not part of the curriculum.

3. **Curriculum involves time.** Curriculum is affected by time in two ways: the time allocated for various topics and activities, and the sequence in which information is taught and learned.

What Is the Purpose of Curriculum?

Curriculum is not simply the stream of events and activities or lessons that occur in a classroom or school. Rather, curriculum is an interrelated set of plans and activities that are intended to result in identifiable *outcomes* that almost always pertain to student learning (Marsh and Willis, 1995). Sometimes these outcomes (or goals) are stated explicitly, as in the case of content and performance standards listed in state or district frameworks. Other times, curricular goals are simply implied, for example, by a teacher's choice of materials or allocation of instructional time.

It is important to remember that curriculum is intended to benefit individual students as well as the greater society in which those students operate. For example, social studies was introduced as a distinct content area during the early part of the 20th century when schools were intended to promote the assimilation of a rapidly growing population that included large numbers of children from rural and immigrant families arriving in the industrial cities. Schools were expected to prepare effective citizens who could take their place as productive members of the American work force. Similarly, science and math curricula frequently were scrutinized and reformed in the 1950s and 1960s when it was believed the United States was lagging behind the Soviet Union in the Cold War and ensuing Space Race. Today standards-based school reform clearly is expected to result in benefits for society by producing workers who will be able to contribute to a 21st century global economy.

Teachers tend to have a very specific view of curriculum and are used to thinking about curriculum in the context of a particular classroom or student. They are primarily concerned with how or what to teach "today," "this week," and "this year." This more immediate perspective results in shorter-term goals. Indeed, some of the tension that has formed around standards-based reform, particularly in the context of special education, is that it is sometimes difficult for teachers to see the benefits for individual students in content and performance standards that may appear to be too academic or cognitively demanding. Yet despite the short-term difficulties involved in teaching these skills, these larger goals may be very important to life-long success. One of the most important purposes of curriculum is to serve as a map that provides information about short-term goals as well as long-term outcomes.

Curriculum as a Map for Teachers

When you use a map to plan a road trip, you always have your eventual destination in mind, but you can't simply draw a straight line from point A to point B. You have to take into account variables such as the location of the specific roads on which you will be traveling, how fast you can travel, and the overall distance you will be covering. Often, you identify interim landmarks that help you decide whether or not you are on the right track.

You can use this same kind of thinking to connect the shorter-term goals of an individual to broader curriculum outcomes. Two things teachers must consider in using curriculum this way are *immediacy* and *specificity*.

Immediacy refers to the settings and timeframe in which curriculum outcomes are expected to occur. Immediate environments are those in which a student is expected to operate frequently, such as their classrooms, playgroups, or homes. Less immediate environments are those in which the student is exposed to only occasionally or those in which a student is expected to perform in the future, such as next year's math class, after graduation from high school, or in the workplace. It is important to remember that most district or state content and performance standards are intended to reflect specific learning that occurs over a period of two to three years. These standards often correspond to when assessments are administered.

As you think about the purpose of curriculum outcomes or goals for a particular individual or class, you must consider how soon you expect the outcome to occur. For special education teachers, that means planning for the immediate classroom environments and current instructional units or lesson plans as well as for the next two to three years when an assessment is administered or other key transitions occur (such as, elementary to middle school, middle to high school, and adulthood). There should be a clear path from the immediate, short-term goals that apply in today's class to the long-term goals you would want the student to accomplish in the long term. Of course, most teachers may find that three to five years is the most distant target for which they can reasonably expect to set goals.

Specificity

The purpose of curriculum may be very specific and focused or it may be more general. For example, a very focused curriculum goal would be for students to learn a specific skill such as single-digit multiplication, while a more diffuse goal would be for students to learn to understand and apply concepts and procedures from number sense. Special education IEP goals tend to be fairly specific, while content standards in most statewide curriculum frameworks tend to be more general. As a rule, the more specific a curriculum outcome is, the more easily it can be broken into teachable steps that can be measured. Yet if we only focus on small steps, we lose the larger focus and the ability to do long-term planning. In other words, it is important not to lose sight of the forest because of the trees. Many states, in their standards developments, have attempted to reach a middle ground between highly specific, observable goals that are readily teachable and the more general statements of outcomes. For example, Kansas uses the descriptors associated with its science standards, shown in Figure 2.1.

Curriculum Involves a Domain

Curriculum is the "what" of schooling; it is the content that teachers teach and that students learn. Curriculum is separate from the strategies (or methods) teachers use to manage and instruct students in the content, although the line between curriculum and instruction often is (and should be) difficult to separate in day-to-day practices. The extent or breadth of specific curriculum content (also called the *scope*) is determined by the nature of the subject matter domain (such as earth science, consumer mathematics, or writing) and the purpose of the curriculum (teaching basic skills or teaching the authentic use of knowledge such as algebra). When the skills and knowledge are defined broadly, or when the purpose is ill-defined, the scope will be less clear. Narrower domains and well-defined purposes generally will limit the scope of a curriculum. For example, the scope of a curriculum intended to "promote moral development" likely would be much broader and less well-defined than that of a curriculum intended to prepare commercial refrigeration technicians. The scope is a horizontal look at the range of courses, topics, or activities within a subject matter across a given time frame or grade level, or across a given student's educational career. A third-grade math curriculum might present a range of topics including single- and two-digit addition, subtraction with regrouping, single-digit multiplication, two-step word problems, proportion, probability, and measurement. These

Figure 2.1   Kansas science standards

Standards: General statements of what students should know, understand, and be able to do in the natural sciences over the course of their K-12 education. The standards are interwoven ideas, not separate entities. Thus, they should be taught as interwoven ideas, not as separate entities. Science standards for the state of Kansas are clustered for grade levels K-2, 3-4, 5-8, and 9-12:

      1. Science as Inquiry
      2. Physical Science
      3. Life Science
      4. Earth and Space Science
      5. Science and Technology
      6. Science in Personal and Environmental Perspectives
      7. History and Nature of Science

Here is the Science as Inquiry standard:

As a result of the activities in grades K-2, all students should experience science as full inquiry. In elementary grades, students begin to develop the physical and intellectual abilities of scientific inquiry.

Benchmarks: Specific statements of what students should know and be able to do at a specified point in their schooling. Benchmarks are used to measure students' progress toward meeting a standard. Benchmarks for the Kansas science standards are defined for grades 2, 4, 8, and 10.

Here is the first Benchmark for the Science as Inquiry standard:

All students will begin to develop abilities necessary to do scientific inquiries. However, not every activity will involve all of these stages, nor must any particular sequences of these stages be followed. Full inquiry involves asking a simple question, completing an investigation, answering the question, and presenting the results to others.

Indicators: Statements of the knowledge or skills that students demonstrate in order to meet a benchmark. Indicators are critical to understanding the standards and benchmarks and are to be met by all students. For the Kansas science standards, the indicators listed under each benchmark are not listed in priority order, nor should the list be considered as all-inclusive. The list of indicators and examples should be considered as representative but not as comprehensive or all-inclusive.

Examples: Two kinds of examples are used in the Kansas science standards. An instructional example offers an activity or a specific concrete instance of an idea of what is called for by an indicator. A clarifying example provides an illustration of the meaning or intent of an indicator. Like the indicators themselves, examples are considered to be representative, but not comprehensive or all-inclusive.

Here are the indicators and examples for the Science as Inquiry Benchmark presented above:

    Indicator: *The student will identify characteristics of objects.*
    Example: *States characteristics of leaves, shells, water, and air.*

    Indicator: *The student will classify and arrange groups of objects by a variety of characteristics.*
    Example: *Groups seeds by color, texture, size; groups objects by whether they float or sink; groups rocks by texture, color, and hardness.*

---

topics would not necessarily all be treated equally during the third-grade year though. Some would be taught to mastery, while others might only be introduced. However, each probably would be addressed in some way at some point during the third-grade year.

Specifying the Domain

The information that makes up curriculum comes in a variety of forms. A number of taxonomies have been suggested over the years to

Figure 2.2   Types of information

Facts are defined as simple associations between names, objects, events, places, and so on that use singular exemplars. Learning facts involves making a consistent connection between a stimulus and a response. This association may simply involve associating a label or name with an object or it may express a relationship between two or more objects or events, such as the phrase "Salem is the capital of Oregon." Because facts describe only one relationship, they may be grouped together in descriptions of unique events, objects, or places. In a chapter in a world geography textbook, a section describing the Indian subcontinent might include specific facts about climate and topography grouped together under the subtitle "The Four Greats of India" (great rivers, great winds, great mountains, and great plateau). However, each individual fact (such as the name of each of the rivers or the location of the great plateau) would need to be taught and remembered as a specific name or place. In this respect, facts may not be difficult to teach or test, but they are especially difficult to learn because they must be memorized and have little explanatory power beyond the specific stimulus-response relationship they describe.

Concepts are clusters of events, names, dates, objects, and places that share a common set of defining attributes or characteristics. A concept may be thought of as a category having a rule that defines its relevant characteristics, a name, and a set of instances or exemplars that share the key attributes. In this definition, rules provide the basis for organizing the attributes of the concept. These attributes, in turn, provide the criteria for distinguishing examples of the concept from non-examples. This is a classical view of concepts that does not cover every contingency likely to be encountered, but it does provide a framework for thinking about content contained in curricula. Many concepts encountered in content classes are quite complex, with conditional or nested attributes or membership in multiple categories.

Principles indicate causal or co-variant relationships among different facts or concepts, more often the latter. A principle usually represents an if-then or cause-effect relationship, although this relationship may not be stated explicitly. A principle generally involves multiple applications in which the fundamental relationship among the relevant concepts is constant across virtually all examples of the concepts. For example, the law of supply and demand can be taught as the principle "when supply goes up, demand goes down," with comparable applications found in the context of medieval European city states, a child's lemonade stand, and the 1929 Stock Market crash.

Procedures involve the steps or phases required to complete a process. For example, the topic "Scientific Method" may be taught in a seventh-grade science class as a series of steps proceeding from the formation of a hypothesis, the construction of an experiment, the collection of data, and the evaluation of results. However, procedural knowledge involves more than simply knowing what the steps are, but focuses on knowing how to execute those steps in an actual experiment (Anderson, 1983). Often, procedures can be formatted as a set of principles that comprise a decision chain of the form "If A occurs, then I do B. If C occurs, then I do D, and so on," with the execution following a series of decisions based on results obtained at each preceding step. For example, writing a research paper might involve a series of decisions about where to obtain information, which information to include, the order in which information should be presented, and so on.

describe the types of information in school curricula, including the well-known ones formulated by Bloom (Bloom et al., 1956) and Gagné (Gagné, Briggs, and Wager, 1988). In general, information in curriculum takes the form of facts, concepts, principles, and procedures. Descriptions of these are shown in Figure 2.2.

It is critical for teachers to understand the underlying structure of the information contained in curriculum for two reasons. First, teachers must design instruction that matches as closely as possible the cognitive processes involved in learning the subject matter. In the next chapter, we will examine those processes and, as you will see, the learning processes depend greatly on the type of information to be learned. For example, the recall of facts involves a different kind of thinking than application of a strategy. Because different kinds of information are learned and remembered differently, they also must be taught differently. Therefore, the success a student experiences in learning the information contained in curriculum depends to a great extent on the teacher's ability to match specific instructional strategies with the content and the purpose or goal of learning that content.

The second reason it is important for teachers to understand the type of the information contained in the curriculum is that the types of information students learn determines the kind of thinking they can do. The more complex the information, the more useful it is for higher-order thinking and problem solving. These require different types of instruction.

Unfortunately, much of what students traditionally have been asked to learn in schools is comprised primarily of facts and simple concepts. However, as we noted in the last chapter, many of the new standards and curriculum in place in schools today require more complex learning. One of the biggest challenges teachers face is to help their students transform facts and simple concepts into principles and procedures. Specifying the domain of the general curriculum involves a process of cataloging the types of information involved (facts, concepts, principles, and procedures), and then prioritizing that information in order of importance for accomplishing the desired outcomes. This prioritization process should be based on teacher domain expertise as well as the specificity and immediacy of expected outcomes.

Curriculum and Time

It is impossible to think about curriculum without thinking about time. Two dimensions of time are of particular concern. The first has to do with the allocation of instructional or learning time to various aspects of the curriculum and the second has to do with the order in which a curriculum presents information and activities over time.

Allocated Time

Allocated time is the time a district, school, or teacher provides for instruction (Berliner, 1990). The time allocated to instruction should be distinguished from *engaged time*, which is the time students actually spend paying attention to materials or activities that have educational goals. Although time allocated may not necessarily translate directly to engaged time, it is a reasonable indicator of the extent to which students have the opportunity to learn in a particular domain. Needless to say, students whose opportunities to receive instruction in a curriculum area are limited because too little time is allocated for instruction would be unlikely to meet challenging performance standards in that area.

Allocated time has additional meaning when we consider students who have learning problems. If our expectation is that a student is going to *attain* a particular curricular goal, rather than simply receive instruction related to it, then we need to ensure that sufficient time is allocated for learning to occur. Of course, all other things being equal, students who have learning problems require more time to learn than their peers. It may be difficult to make the claim that a student who has learning problems has had an *adequate* opportunity to learn if insufficient time is allocated to accommodate her or his specific learning needs.

The time allocated to various aspects of the curriculum generally reflects an ordering of instructional priorities. More time is usually allocated to those curriculum areas that are of a higher priority to a district, school, or teacher. For example, in elementary school, a large proportion of the day is allocated to reading and writing instruction because learning to read and write are viewed as the most important outcomes for students at that level. In later grades, more time is allocated to other topics as the focus shifts from basic skills to more subject matter content instruction.

Two common problems associated with prioritizing curriculum are *overload* and *omission*. When the scope of the curriculum is too wide (when we try to squeeze too much information into the curriculum), students do not have enough time to learn, known as an *overloaded curriculum*. Curricula that suffer from this problem often are described as being a mile wide and an inch deep. There are many topics, but little depth or mastery of subject matter. This is a problem of many curriculum programs used in the United States. In an attempt to be all things to all users, textbooks often include far too much information about a given topic. Teachers who fail to make thoughtful choices about which aspects of the subject matter to address may end up overloading the curriculum. The chief dilemma resulting from this problem is the lack of instructional time available to help students learn the material. Teachers often are reduced to simply mentioning or glossing over subject matter.

The second problem involves curriculum omissions. Each time a teacher makes the decision to include or emphasize some piece of information, they also make an implicit decision not to include other things. For example, if, over the course of a year-long sixth-grade language arts class, a teacher spends relatively more instructional time teaching a generic writing process, relatively little time may be allocated to instruction on strategies for writing research papers. If students never have the opportunity to learn how to write research papers, the omission of this skill from the curriculum would be problematic later on when more technical writing is required.

Curriculum Sequence

Sequence refers to the order in which a curriculum presents information and activities over time, either within or across school years. Knowing how a particular curriculum is sequenced can help teachers avoid the problems of curriculum overloading or curriculum omission. They must establish priorities about what to include in the curriculum. A number of organizing strategies can be used to sequence curriculum information (Armstrong, 1989; Posner and Strike, 1976; Smith and Ragan, 1999). Some commonly used sequencing strategies are outlined here.

Thematic Sequencing

Topics are organized so that the skills and knowledge associated with separate themes are taught together. For example, a middle school general science class might include the separate themes of electricity, magnetism, plate tectonics, ecology, and human systems. With thematic sequencing, each thematic unit stands alone. Knowing the information associated with one theme may not lead to a better understanding of the next theme to be taught. For example, knowing how *s waves* and *p waves*, function in an earthquake wouldn't necessarily help a student learn about the respiratory system.

Task Analytic Sequencing

This sequencing strategy attempts to build on a learner's increasing store of prior knowledge. Prerequisite information is presented first and then this information is built upon in later instruction. This sequencing strategy also might be thought of as a *part to whole* strategy or *bottom up* approach. This classic task analysis approach to curriculum sequencing generally is associated with behavioral views of learning and can be found in a wide variety of applications in special education as well as general education content. For example, in math, students would be taught simple addition and subtraction facts first, and then use this information to solve two-step word problems later on.

Just-in-Time Sequencing

Topics are taught according to the order in which the students need them. Information that is needed soonest is taught first. Information that is needed later is taught "just in time" for the learner to use it. For example, students might be taught to decode or sight-read a small set of high-frequency words early in a beginning reading curricula. Later on, less frequently encountered words would be taught as they occur in the reading material the students encounter.

Whole-to-Part Sequencing

This sequencing strategy presents general information first, and then later, more specific information is introduced. This strategy is more or less the opposite of the Task Analytic approach described previously. For example, in a science class, students might first learn about general life systems such as respiration and reproduction, and then learn about the parts and functions of plant and animal cells. In math, students might learn to develop their own approach to solving problems using manipulatives before they learn to do the specific computations involved. The Whole-to-Part sequencing strategy is closely associated with constructivist and cognitive views of learning.

Decisions About Time

In practice, curriculum and instruction usually involve a blending of sequencing strategies. For example, to teach beginning reading, an effective teacher may teach decoding as a prerequisite skill (Task Analytic approach), teach frequently occurring words as sight words (Just-In-Time approach), and employ a combination of written and oral language activities that enable students to gain a holistic view of what reading entails (Whole-to-Part approach).

It is important to consider the scope as well as short- and long-term goals of curriculum when deciding how to sequence information to ensure that students have an adequate opportunity to learn the things we want them to know by the time they need to know it. Teachers also must avoid curriculum omissions that will place a student at a disadvantage later on. However, it is critical that teachers not get stuck in the idea of "readiness" as they make decisions about time and curriculum. Many students who have learning problems require consistent, direct instruction and many trials to learn important basic skills such as reading and computation. These students may never have the opportunity to work toward the challenging outcomes contained in the curriculum frameworks if they are not deemed "ready" to move on until they have learned basic readiness skills. Teachers must consider the long- and short-term goals of curriculum, along with the sequencing strategies to avoid the "ready means never" dilemma.

Finding the General Curriculum

The nature of curriculum is such that it is nearly impossible to identify the definitive general curriculum. What constitutes the general curriculum depends on the perspective from which it is viewed, the outcomes that are expected, and the manner in which it is implemented in the classroom. However, a clear expectation exists in IDEA-97 as well as federal and state policies associated with standards-based reform that students who have disabilities will have meaningful access to the curriculum in which their nondisabled peers receive instruction. At the same time, the long-standing traditions of equal protection and the provision of an appropriate individualized education program are still central to

IDEA. These seemingly competing demands will require teachers to pursue a thoughtful and comprehensive analysis of the core curriculum elements discussed in this chapter: purpose, domain, and time.

In this chapter, we have discussed these core elements as separate entities, but in reality, curriculum involves a complex interaction of these components. Therefore, the process of finding the general curriculum requires a multidimensional thinking strategy. The thinking and planning process involved in finding the general curriculum is illustrated in Figure 2.3 and discussed in the following section.

The process of sorting out the complex and dynamic mix of curriculum elements to find the general curriculum requires a "triage" mindset. The most pressing or urgent needs must be addressed first, and then secondary and tertiary curriculum goals are established. The goals of the general curriculum will be different for different individuals or groups. Special education generally is concerned with the needs of individual students, but planning for an individual student must take place within the larger context of the curriculum outcomes expected for all students. In Chapter 5, "Access to Curriculum and the Individual Education Program," we will discuss the process of linking the larger context of curriculum to the specific

Figure 2.3   Finding the general curriculum

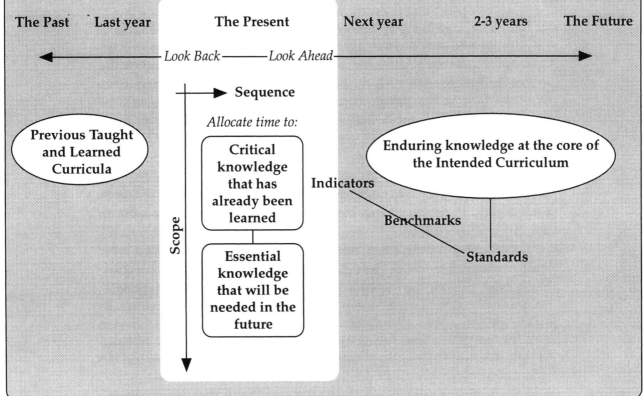

needs of an individual student in the IEP process. We'll confine our discussion here to identifying what it is all students will be expected to learn.

The Present

Time is the overarching organizing structure within which the general curriculum is to be found. We view the curriculum through the continuously moving window of the present to conduct a forward- and backward-looking analysis and decide how curricular time should be allocated. Specifically, we want to know *what should be taught* and *in what sequence it should be taught*. This is where the triage approach comes in. Of all the information that potentially could be included in the curriculum, what is the *most* important? Remember, be aware of seductive details and curriculum overload. Just because a publisher included some esoteric bit of information in a textbook does not mean you need to allocate valuable curriculum time to it.

For any particular student or group of students, these questions of what to teach and when to teach it require identification of the essential knowledge that will be needed in the future as well as the critical knowledge that has already been learned. Of course, these two pieces of information are linked, but the starting point for this analysis lies in the future.

Looking Ahead and Looking Back

The most important decision in finding the general curriculum is to identify the enduring knowledge that is at the core of the intended curriculum: standards, benchmarks and indicators. As we discussed earlier in this chapter, the standards entail a broader scope and are anchored two to three years in the future. Benchmarks are narrower and would be accomplished sooner, while indicators are immediate and specific. However, curriculum standards do not exist as isolated or arbitrary. Curriculum standards are situated in the larger context of the knowledge domains from which they are sampled. For example, a standard that requires students to "use geographic tools such as maps and charts to understand the spatial arrangement of people, places, and resources on the Earth" has relevance beyond the simple task of locating specific places on a map during a test. Rather, the point of such a standard is for students to learn to "think like a geographer" (Harper, 1990) and to eventually have informed opinions about issues such as population growth, the protection of endangered species, global warming, or geopolitics. In other words, the general curriculum is not just specific goals contained in a set of guidelines established by the state. It represents a meaningful sample of a much larger knowledge domain that extends far beyond the context the classroom.

Clearly then, identifying the enduring knowledge associated with the intended curriculum requires a deep understanding of the disciplines. Educators who have only a superficial understanding of a particular domain associated with the intended curriculum will be unable to engage in this analysis and should seek the assistance of content specialists. Of course, few teachers would be expected to have extensive expertise in more than a few domains, so finding the general curriculum almost certainly requires a collaborative process among thoughtful, knowledgeable teachers.

The desired outcome of this process is a set of clear statements delineating the most critical knowledge that all students will be expected to learn as a result of working in the curriculum and the approximate timeframe in which the student would need to have acquired the knowledge. This list need not be exhaustive, but it should fairly represent the most enduring, salient knowledge all students will need to learn. This knowledge then becomes the top priority in the curriculum triage.

A word of caution is needed here though. Although we just said that some degree of content expertise is required in this process, be careful not to create a list of the knowledge that is required to *become* a content expert. Again, be careful to avoid curriculum overload. It is not necessary for everyone who studies history, mathematics, geography, or science in school to become a historian, mathematician, geographer, or scientist. The goal is to provide all students with access to the information they will need to become effective members of society and to peruse a variety of post-school options. Further study in the disciplines is only one of those options.

When the enduring knowledge that all students must learn has been clarified, it is possible to start mapping backward from the future to the present to decide what will be needed in the future that has not been learned yet. This final step in finding the general curriculum entails looking back at previously taught curricula as well as evaluation of the learned curriculum to decide how to allocate curriculum time in the present. At this point, it is important to consider any sequencing strategies that were used in previously taught curricula as well as the actual learned curricula students bring with them to the present.

For groups of students, this analysis can focus on documents, curriculum materials, and teacher judgment. However, in the context of special education, it is likely that there will be a concern with the prior knowledge and future needs of a particular student. We will discuss the assessment process necessary for selecting curriculum goals for individual students in Chapter 4, "Evaluating the Outcomes of Access," and we will present a strategy for thinking about how the IEP relates to the general curriculum in Chapter 5.

Chapter Summary

Here is a summary of the key points we discussed in this chapter:

* The general curriculum includes the full range of courses, activities, lessons, and materials used routinely by the general population of a school.

- The *intended* curriculum is the official or adopted curriculum, often contained in state or district policy. This is the body of content that students are expected to learn as a result of their school experiences.

- The *taught* curriculum is the minute-to-minute, day-to-day, and week-to-week events that actually occur in the classroom. It includes teacher instructional behaviors such as questioning or lecturing as well as the curriculum materials used in a classroom.

- The *learned* curriculum is what students actually learn as a result of being in the classroom and interacting with the intended and taught curricula.

- The purpose of curriculum is to bring about desired outcomes. These outcomes may take the form of short-term goals or long-term expectations.

- Specification of the curriculum domain defines the limits of what is and what is not part of the curriculum. The information contained in curriculum takes on various forms that each require different instructional considerations.

- Time allocation is an indication of curriculum priorities. Sufficient time must be allocated to provide students with an adequate opportunity to learn the content contained in the curriculum.

- Decisions about what to include or exclude from curriculum must take into account the sequencing strategy that underlies the curriculum. False assumptions that a particular topic will be taught later on in the curriculum can lead to curriculum omissions. Overemphasis of "readiness skills" will lead to the "ready means never" dilemma.

3

THE LEARNING-TEACHING CONNECTION

Research conducted in the past few decades has led to new understandings of the fundamentals of human learning. Numerous studies and much scholarly debate have focused on critical questions about how memory works, how people transfer what they have learned across situations, and how "experts" differ from "novices" in the way they use knowledge.

One of the most direct results of this research on learning is that the notion of what it means to be a teacher has changed considerably in recent years. We now understand that truly effective teachers are able to make crucial links between *curriculum* and *instruction* by attending to the way their students learn. We no longer think of teachers as mere ciphers who simply transmit facts because the focus in schools has shifted from drill, practice, and rote learning to promoting students' understanding and use of subject matter content. Moreover, we now know that being an effective teacher involves more than simply having a large toolbox of teaching techniques that are applied indiscriminately across content. The research has shown the importance of providing opportunities for students to *use*, rather than simply *acquire*, information.

This chapter presents an overview of the recent research on how people learn. The reason we have devoted an entire chapter to this topic is that this growing body of knowledge is fundamentally changing what it means to access the curriculum. We will examine some of the critical processes involved in learning and memory, and we will look at the ways in which teachers can enhance student learning by designing instruction that supports those processes. After reading this chapter, you may also want to consult some of the resources listed in the Appendix for additional information on this subject.

Learning Research and Implications for Teaching

Beginning in the late 1950s, researchers began to view human learning as the active processing of information, rather than simply responding to stimuli. This idea led to the development of a conceptual model of learning in which information is processed through separate memory systems (Atkinson and Shiffrin, 1968). This view differed considerably from the stimulus-response theories of learning that dominated in the first half of the 20th century.

This *information-processing* model of learning has been extremely influential in generating research on the way humans learn and remember.[1] The findings from this research are beginning to exert a profound influence on both curriculum and instruction (Bransford, Brown, and Cocking, 1999), as well as the various curriculum frameworks being implemented in schools today. For example, some of the new assessments associated with the new content and performance standards tend to emphasize problem-solving in real-life contexts, rather than just recalling facts (McDonnell, McLaughlin, and Morrison, 1997; Thurlow, 1994). As curricula and expectations for student achievement have begun to more directly reflect the modern understanding of learning, the challenge for teachers seeking to help all students access the general curriculum is becoming clear. Teachers must be able to design instruction in specific content areas that addresses three fundamental processes: memory, the skilled use of knowledge, and generalization and transfer.

Instruction that emphasizes these fundamental learning processes is particularly important for students who have learning problems. For example, students who have learning disabilities tend to make poor use of learning strategies such as rehearsal and planning (Torgesen, 1982) and they often have poor skills in remembering language (Deshler, Warner, Schumaker, and Alley, 1983). These deficits in turn often lead to deficien-

---

[1]Other theories of learning based on *connectionist* models and *constructivist* philosophy have also gained much attention and popularity in recent years and merit serious scholarly consideration. However, the information-processing model of learning has been researched extensively for over 30 years and has resulted in the development of robust instructional applications. Because more recent models of learning and memory have not yet resulted in a coherent body of empirically validated instructional practice, we have limited our discussion primarily to the implications of information processing research.

cies in general knowledge. However, considerable evidence shows that the performance of students with learning problems can be improved when they are provided with supports for storing and retrieving information (Hallahan, Kauffman, and Lloyd, 1996). To show how teachers can build these supports into instruction, we will take a closer look at the processes involved in learning and memory.

How Information Is Processed and Remembered

Skilled learners often are described in terms of superior recall, both in terms of what they remember (Glaser and Chi, 1988) and how they recognize patterns in information (Bransford et al., 1986). Research has demonstrated that recall is not simply a matter of hours of drill or experience with a set of facts or skills (de Groot, 1965). Rather, recall is related to how efficiently a learner has stored information into long-term memory. This in turn is very much related to the structure of the underlying knowledge and experience the learner has had with similar information. The more prior knowledge a person has in a particular area, the better able they are to recognize patterns and organize a structure for all similar or related knowledge about the same topic. Without such a structure, a learner must deal with new facts and concepts as individual pieces of information, instead of part of a pattern. This is time-consuming and, as subject matter becomes more difficult, can soon overwhelm the student's memory capacity.

Figure 3.1 shows a schematic of the major components of the *information processing* model of learning. The components illustrated in Figure 3.1 refer to activities the brain conducts as it processes and stores information. These processes will be discussed in the following section.

Figure 3.1   The information processing model of learning and memory

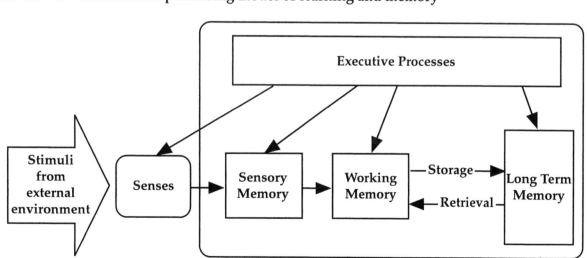

Sensory Memory

As a stimulus (or information) from the environment is detected through one of the senses, it is held briefly in *sensory memory* until it can be analyzed. This analysis involves two activities: the allocation of *attention* to the stimulus and *recognition*, the process of matching the incoming stimulus with a recognizable pattern already stored in memory.

To allocate attention to something, a student must select it from among many sensory inputs that occur simultaneously. Teachers can assist students in this process by limiting the amount of information to which they ask students to attend at any one time. For example, teachers who use clear, concise wording in their presentations often are better able to maintain and focus student attention than those who require their students to pick the most important information out of an endless stream of superfluous "happy talk." The idea is to say less but make every word count.

Recognition is an automatic activity that is enhanced by prior knowledge. For example, a novice reader might not notice the letter *e* at the end of the word *bake*, but a skilled reader would more likely attend to it. Similarly, a skilled speaker of English might more readily perceive and recognize the spoken phoneme /v/ than would someone who speaks American Spanish as their first language.

Sensory memory has an extremely limited capacity. Visual information begins to fade after only one-half of a second and auditory stimuli are held for only about three seconds. Information that has been perceived and recognized in sensory memory is passed on to the *working memory*, but stimuli that aren't attended to or aren't recognized fade away quickly and are replaced by new incoming information. Effective teachers recognize this problem and use a variety of strategies to focus and maintain student attention and aid in recognition. Here are some classroom strategies that can promote attention and recognition:

- **Establish and keep schedules of classroom activities and events, and provide systematic reminders for students of the sequence in which activities will occur.** For example, post the daily schedule on the blackboard and then periodically remind students to consult the schedule to see what is coming up next. This strategy cuts down on transition time and helps students focus their attention more quickly after a transition has been made.

- **Use a consistent set of signals to cue student attention.** Signals used with younger children can include bells, hand-claps, verbal cues (such as "Eyes on me"), or turning lights on and off. Older students may be cued with more subtle but consistent signals such as standing in front of the class to begin each new activity, turning the overhead projector on, or age-appropriate verbal cues (such as "OK, now listen up").

- **Use clear, concise directions that focus on only one task at a time.** For example, use short, specific directions such as "Turn to page 73." Wait until everyone has turned to the correct page and then say, "Everyone, look at the problems on the bottom of page 73." Pause and then say, "Do the problems on the bottom of page 73 and show your work," rather than giving complex, multi-step directions such as "Do the problems at the bottom of page 73 and be sure to show your work. Then when you have finished those, you may work on the challenge problem on the board or else finish your journal writing from before."

* **Plan tasks according to the amount of attention required to complete them.** If a task is too long or requires students to attend to too many variables, their attention may drift. Break up lessons into smaller segments with different but related activities that require a variety of responses. For example, a math problem-solving lesson might start with a large group presentation and modeling, followed by a partner task using manipulatives, followed by a task students complete individually at their desk, followed by a group presentation and questioning to wrap up the lesson. Depending on the age of the students, each segment might last from eight to 10 minutes. Of course, the transitions between lesson segments would need to be cued as we discussed previously so that the students are told what they should be doing and to which aspects of the task they should be attending.

* **Use a variety of types of questions to aid recognition.** Student attention waivers quickly if they are not challenged by teacher questioning or if the questions are too difficult. Ask a variety of related questions that require students to recall declarative information, make inferences, form opinions, and make evaluations. Also, avoid guessing games. Only ask questions that you think your students know how to answer.

* **Present information in more than one format.** This strategy assists students in attending to and recognizing salient information in instruction by focusing their attention on what is similar in the two formats (Case, 1985). Examples of this strategy include the use of manipulatives to model math concepts, laboratory demonstrations to illustrate chemistry or physics problems, step-by-step illustrated descriptions of math problem-solving steps, and teacher think-alouds paired with a demonstration of how to write a compare-contrast paragraph.

* **Employ brisk lesson pacing and provide frequent opportunities for students to respond.** Choral responding can be used even with older students when it is embedded in age-appropriate and respectful contexts. Similarly, students can write responses on small, white boards with erasable pens and then quickly hold them up during group lessons.

* **Frequently check to be sure your students are attending and understand your expectations.** Ask questions that require students to demonstrate understanding and attention rather than yes/no questions. For example, ask, "Bonnie, on what page are we all going to be working?" rather than "Bonnie, are you on the correct page?"

Working Memory

As soon as a learner recognizes a stimulus in sensory memory, that stimulus is passed on to working memory so that meaning can be attached to it. Information is held in working memory temporarily while it is compared with information already stored in long-term memory. If the new information is related to some prior knowledge, it is moved out of working memory and stored along with that related information in long-term memory. At the same time, the nature of what is already stored in long-term memory changes to accommodate the newly learned information. This process is illustrated in Figure 3.2.

If the new information cannot be connected to prior knowledge, it is less likely to be moved into long-term memory. Learners who have a large, well-organized, readily accessible store of prior knowledge in long-term memory are better able to process information through working memory than those who lack prior knowledge or are less able to access information stored in long-term memory.

Working memory also has a very limited capacity. Only about seven units of information can be held there at one time, for about 10 to 20 seconds. Information is lost from working memory as a result of interference from new stimuli. As newer information is moved into working memory, it "overwrites" what is already there much the same way a computer file can be overwritten by a newer version. Information can be retained for longer periods of time in working memory through rehearsal. Repeating information aloud or subvocally has the effect of continually refreshing the information in working memory before it can be interfered with by other stimuli.

It also is possible to increase the amount of information that can be processed in working memory by *chunking* smaller bits of information into larger units. For example, a 10-digit telephone number is easier to

Figure 3.2   Linking new information with prior knowledge

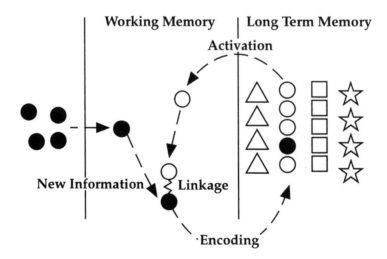

remember when it is chunked into three units of the configuration: (xxx) xxx-xxxx. Chunking is particularly useful for helping learners store declarative knowledge in long-term memory, especially when they have little prior knowledge with which to work. Chunking has the effect of simplifying the cognitive load by imposing meaning on otherwise disconnected bits of information. Later recall also is simplified because the learner only has to activate the first item in the chain to recall the entire sequence. Here are some classroom strategies to help students manage working memory:

* **Organize the information you want your students to learn before you teach it.** Use advance organizers and graphic displays to show the structure of the information to be learned. When information can be organized into categories, show the superordinate and subordinate relationships among various elements of what you want your students to learn. When declarative knowledge can be chunked into meaningful clusters, make the chunking scheme explicit for students during instruction, rather than relying on them to make the links on their own.

* **Provide direct assistance to help students activate prior knowledge already stored in long-term memory.** Many teachers use a variety of techniques designed to stimulate recall, such as strategic questioning and recall diagrams. Never assume that students have fully learned what you may think they have learned or that they will be able to recall that information when they need it. You can facilitate recall directly by explicitly telling students what you want them to think about prior to the presentation of new information. For example, use statements such as this to prompt recall. "Yesterday we learned that zero is the identity function in addition. Think about what happens when you add zero to a number. It stays the same. Today we will learn about the identity function in multiplication. What do you think will happen when we multiply a number by the identity function?"

* **Help students make links between old and new information.** Various associational techniques include mnemonics, analogies, and imagery. However, learners who lack sufficient prior knowledge or whose long-term memory is poorly organized may experience great difficulty connecting new with old information on their own. Sometimes simply telling students how the new information you want them to learn is related to knowledge they already have is the most effective way to facilitate linkage.

* **Incorporate elaboration tactics into your instruction.** These tactics prompt students to think about new and previously learned information at the same time. Prompt students to paraphrase or summarize what they have learned in their own words. Provide students with structured study guides or note-taking supports that prompt simultaneous attention to old

and new information. For example, students learning how to compute area might be prompted on a study guide to tell how the computation of area is similar to the computation of perimeter (assuming the computation of perimeter is prior knowledge). We will discuss elaboration in a little more detail later in this chapter.

Storage and Retrieval

In the learning and memory process, information flows in two directions between working and long-term memory. The storage of new information in long-term memory (a process known as *encoding*) is probably the most important component of the learning process. Information that has been encoded effectively is more likely to be remembered (*retrieved*) than information that is not stored properly. Two key variables affect how well information is stored in and retrieved from long-term memory: frequency and meaningfulness. The more often information is encountered, the more likely it is to be easily retrieved when needed. This is why it is important for teachers to provide opportunities for their students to practice using recently learned information. Practice sessions can be either *massed* or *distributed*.

Massed practice involves longer sessions of intense practice at irregular intervals. Cramming on the night before a test is an example of massed practice. *Distributed practice* refers to regularly scheduled practice sessions that may be shorter and less intense than massed practice. In general, distributed practice is much more effective than massed practice because it increases the frequency with which a learner encounters the to-be-learned information and activates relevant prior knowledge in long-term memory. Teachers can facilitate this process by systematically building in short practice sessions throughout the day and over subsequent days following the introduction of new information.

Distributed practice also is important for building automaticity and fluency. Being fluent does not always mean being fast. It does, however, mean that the learner does not have to focus concentrated attention on trying to remember what to do. Fluency increases as a learner gains more experience with a task. For example, a beginning reader must struggle with the decoding of every word because they have not learned letter-sound associations that fluent readers make automatically. Fluency is important because a person can only consciously attend a finite amount of information at any one time. A child who is struggling with basic word recognition cannot attend to all of the nuances of a paragraph or the concepts and principles being presented.

Two situations can interfere with the storage of new information in long-term memory: when the learner lacks prior knowledge and when the learner's long-term memory is poorly organized. We will discuss both of these problems in the next section.

Long-Term Memory

Long-term memory is where information is stored permanently. Remembering is the process of locating and *activating* information stored in long-term memory and moving it back into working memory so it can be used. Information is stored in long-term memory with other related information in much the same way material is stored in a library. For example, suppose you go to the library to find the best time to plant dahlias in your region. You would know to look in the area of the library dedicated to horticulture and gardening, rather than the section dedicated to psychology. Similarly, information about dahlias would be stored in your long-term memory "near" other information about gardening, such as the name of your favorite tulip and the type of soil favored by blue hydrangeas.

When the learner does not have relevant prior knowledge to which the new information can be connected, it will seem meaningless and therefore not be remembered. New information enters working memory, but it quickly is forgotten.

When a student lacks sufficient prior knowledge to make a connection with new information being taught, the teacher must provide temporary supports, often called *scaffolding*, to augment the student's existing knowledge. Once the student has enough relevant information stored in long-term memory, the scaffolding can be removed. Scaffolding is a way of systematically transferring control of the skill or knowledge from the teacher to the student. Box 3.1 presents some guidelines for evaluating the quality of scaffolding in a lesson.

Organization of Long-Term Memory

Memory is much more than simple associations. Instead, learners develop structures and schemes for organizing information in long-term memory. These structures govern comprehension as well as how efficiently the learner uses what they already know. Failures can occur if the learner's long-term memory is poorly organized. Then it is more difficult for the learner to activate relevant old knowledge and connect it with new information. If no meaning can be attached to the new information, it fades from working memory, or it is connected to the wrong information in long-term memory, leading to the development of misunderstanding or mistakes. For example, suppose a student learned a set of disconnected facts about the U.S. states (there are 50 states, each has a capital, some were the original 13 colonies). Later, when presented with new examples of government structures associated with the U.S. (such as Puerto Rico and Guam), the student develops the misconception that they must be separate countries, because they are not states.

The organization of long-term memory is one of the key differences between "experts" and "novices." Although experts do have more background knowledge and experience, the real advantage they have over

Box 3.1   Guidelines for Evaluating the Quality of Scaffolding

Kaméenui and Simmons (1999) provide the following guidelines for evaluating the quality of the scaffolding in instruction:

1. The instruction should provide multiple examples of the target skill or information. These examples should be sequenced and juxtaposed so that the student can focus on the most salient features of what it is to be learned.

2. Instruction should begin with easy tasks and progress to more complex tasks as the learner develops more relevant and elaborate prior knowledge.

3. Multiple skills or pieces of information that are likely to be confused should be separated. Introduce one and delay introducing the second until the learner is firm on the first. If you doubt the importance of this guideline, think about how often young children confuse left and right when they have been taught the two concepts at the same time in a "This is my left hand; this is my right hand" format.

4. Introduce only a manageable amount of information. It is far better to break large, complex information up into smaller segments and teach less during multiple lessons than to try to teach everything all at once. One of the most important skills in teaching is knowing how much to teach and at what pace to teach it.

5. Provide enough explicit models of how to use the skill or knowledge being taught. When students lack prior knowledge, they may not know what the correct use of the information looks like. For example, we would not expect someone to learn how to play a musical instrument if they had never heard someone else play it, yet teachers frequently ask their students to perform new, complex tasks with few if any models of correct performance.

6. Provide adequate opportunities for guided practice before a student is required to use a skill or information independently. During guided practice, the learner uses the skill or information under close supervision, and the teacher provides immediate feedback to correct errors and support correct performance. Generally, students should be about 80 percent accurate under guided practice before they are required to perform independently.

novices is that they organize information in long-term memory more efficiently. Experts can analyze and remember larger chunks of information because they store information in categories rather than as separate bits of information. Experts can also process information faster than novices because they can search long-term memory more efficiently.

For example, studies in the area of physics have demonstrated that, when asked to solve problems, beginning students rely on formulas, while experienced students or teachers quickly move to link the problem to certain principles or laws. In the area of history, research conducted by Wineburg (1991) compared high school students' knowledge to that of actual historians on a series of tasks. High school students actually remembered more dates than the experts, but the latter were far superior in elaborating or explaining certain events and in using different approaches to thinking about the problem.

The key to helping students develop an improved organizational strategy is the underlying structure of the information to be stored. Different types of information are stored and retrieved differently in long-term memory. Generally, information stored in long-term memory takes the form of *declarative* knowledge, *procedural* knowledge, or *conditional* knowledge. Declarative knowledge involves "knowing that something is." Procedural knowledge involves "knowing how" to do something, and conditional knowledge involves "knowing when" to do something. Declarative knowledge consists of facts, simple concepts, and beliefs. Procedural knowledge involves more complex concepts, rules, and procedures. Learning strategies associated with executive processes involve both procedural and conditional knowledge. Experts tend to store and retrieve information in networks consisting of interconnected concepts, rules, and procedures, rather than as separate facts. In other words, they make better use of procedural and conditional knowledge.

Teachers can help their students employ more expert storage strategies when they are clear about the kind of information they want their students to learn and the manner in which students will be asked to use that information. The format of the information you want to teach determines your choice of instructional strategy. The key elements of instruction for teaching each type of information are summarized in Table 3.1.

Executive Processes

The *executive processes* control the movement of information through the memory system. Executive control enables the learner to consciously regulate the thinking processes, behaviors, and performances on various tasks. These executive functions include being able to break tasks into manageable steps, organize time to plan ahead, and explain to one's self how to move through a task. Executive processes function like a traffic manager that monitors and controls each of the information-processing structures to facilitate learning. Learners who have well-developed executive processes can handle a greater quantity of information traffic and more complex forms of information. Less skilled learners have less well-developed traffic management systems so they may have more information traffic jams and pile-ups, and information gets lost more often.

Executive process are not automatic but must be activated by the learner. This function is often referred to as *metacognition* or *self-regulation* and generally involves the use of learned strategies. Self-regulation requires a learner to (a) be aware of what strategies or resources a learning task requires, (b) know how and when to use those strategies, and (c) be motivated to use the strategies. A number of specific strategies intended to help students regulate their own learning have been described in the literature in recent years and a full description of them is beyond the scope of this chapter. However, most strategies fall into one of the major categories described by Weinstein and Mayer (1986) and summarized here.

Rehearsal

Rehearsal strategies are intended to help the learner attend to information to be learned and then actively transfer that information into long-term memory. Earlier in this chapter, we noted that rehearsal has the

Table 3.1   Instruction to Teach Various Types of Information

Information Type	Cognitive Tasks Performed by Learner	Implications for Teaching
Facts	• Move information from working memory to long-term memory • Recall information on demand • Link new information with prior knowledge	• Organize information prior to teaching through chunking • Build-in sufficient practice • Build elaboration into later instructional sequences
Concepts	• Discriminate examples from nonexamples of concept class • Generate new examples not previously encountered • Use a model-lead-practice format for instruction	• Carefully select examples and non-examples • Juxtapose examples to focus on salient features
Rules	• Discern multiple parts of the rule relationship • Predict outcomes from part of rule • Discriminate occasions when rule applies	• Teach each part of the rule • Show relationship among rule parts • Incorporate expanded examples into later instructional sequences
Strategies	• Recall component parts of strategy • Recognize occasions when the strategy is useful • Initiate strategy when needed • Evaluate use of strategy through self-monitoring	• Teach each of the component parts of the strategy • Model the strategy and lead learner through use • Show occasions when strategy is useful

effect of increasing the amount of time information is held in working memory so that it can be linked to prior knowledge already stored in long-term memory. Rehearsal strategies can focus on simple or complex learning tasks. Rehearsal strategies for learning simple information (facts such as dates or simple concepts such as shapes or colors) generally involve active repetition of information presented during instruction. Rehearsal strategies for learning more complex information (such as expository material presented in a social studies textbook) can include repeating the material aloud, copying the material, taking detailed notes, and underlining important passages.

Students often need to be taught both *how* and *when* to use rehearsal strategies. Children in the primary grades do not spontaneously use rehearsal, even for learning basic information. Teachers of children at these grades should model simple rehearsal strategies and then explicitly instruct students to use them at appropriate times. By fifth grade, students may spontaneously use some rehearsal but do not possess sufficient background knowledge to do so effectively. For example, they may not be able to accurately discriminate the most important information in a textbook passage (Brown, 1980). Teachers can support students' use of rehearsal strategies to learn more complex information by explicitly instructing them to use the strategy, providing structured note-taking guides and by modeling specific strategies such as repeating important information aloud at the end of a passage.

Elaboration

Elaboration strategies are aimed at helping the learner build meaningful connections between new information to be learned and existing prior knowledge. Elaboration takes place when the learner thinks about new information to be learned and prior knowledge to which it is to be linked at the same time. When the two pieces of information are present together in working memory, the learner can see how the old and new information are related and thus strengthen the connection between them. Elaboration can involve any of a variety of mechanisms for adding to the information to be learned so that it is more easily connected to prior knowledge. Elaboration helps the learner form links within their existing knowledge base to "fill in the gaps."

Elaboration strategies can be used when learning simple or more complex information. When learning simple information such as labels and names or lists of facts, students could write or say sentences that would make the simple fact more meaningful (Smith and Ragan, 1999). For example, students learning the name of the original 13 U.S. colonies might write or orally present sentences that tell the origins of each colony name. Elaboration strategies for learning more complex information can include creating analogies and metaphors, using imagery, answering multi-level questions (literal and inferential, for example), and various note-taking systems. Note-taking and study guides should teach students to distinguish between superordinate and subordinate information and to paraphrase or summarize information in their own words. Mnemonics also are a commonly used and effective elaboration strategy. Again, because students do not spontaneously generate and use these strategies, teachers often must provide explicit instructions about how and when to use them.

Organization

Organizational strategies are aimed at helping the learner structure the information to be learned and then efficiently store it in long-term memory by connecting it to relevant prior knowledge. Clustering or chunking information into categories is the most common organizing strategy for learning simple information. Although most skilled learners do this almost automatically, younger students or students who have learning problems often need to be taught how and when to use this strategy. Teachers can scaffold organizational strategies by arranging information into logical categories prior to instruction, by modeling and leading students through a process of categorizing information, and by pointing out patterns that may exist in the to-be-learned information. Other common strategies for organizing information include the use of graphic organizers, chapter outlines, and expository summaries that show relationships among the information to be learned (Dimino, Gersten, Carnine, and Blake, 1990). For example, students might summarize cause-effect, chronological, or problem solution patterns in passages from textbooks (Armbruster and Anderson, 1985). Teachers can facilitate students' use of organizational strategies by modeling and leading students through outline techniques, providing outlining worksheets in various forms of completion, or by providing blank graphic organizers as study aids prior to reading.

Comprehension Monitoring

When using comprehension monitoring strategies, the learner engages in active and ongoing self-checking to determine how well information is being understood and connected with prior knowledge. Comprehension monitoring involves identifying learning goals (particularly reading) and evaluating the degree to which those goals are being met. Some common and effective monitoring strategies include self-questioning, rereading, paraphrasing, and checking for inconsistencies (Schunk, 1999). Teachers can scaffold students' use of monitoring strategies by modeling the process in "think-aloud" lessons, and by breaking reading tasks into smaller segments and then periodically guiding the student to ask questions about the reading. Pre-during-post reading guides such as K-W-L (What do I *Know*, What do I *Want* to Learn, and What did I *Learn*) questions also aid comprehension monitoring.

Affect

Affective strategies are aimed at helping the student approach learning tasks in a relaxed, positive state of mind and to be effective during studying and learning activities. Common affective strategies include goal-setting and time management activities, reducing external distractions by establishing a common time and place for studying, and the use of self-verbalizations to overcome negative attributions or expectations about learning. Box 3.2 outlines a process for teaching strategies.

Problem-Solving and Transfer

It is clear that teachers can optimize their students' learning by designing instruction that is directed at the underlying learning processes involved in the storage and recall of information from long-term memory. However, success in school entails more than simply remembering things. Students must be able to use information to *solve problems* and they must be able to *transfer* what they have learned to new situations. In the remainder of the chapter, we will discuss ways teachers can design instruction that enhances these two critical learning functions.

Problem-Solving

A problem exists when the way a person wants things to be (a goal) differs from the way they are currently. Of course, much of what constitutes school performance involves solving problems in all subject areas. For example, in math, students solve word problems; in lab sciences, students set up and conduct experiments; and in social studies, students engage in a variety of problem-based activities. Problem-solving is also a key feature of most state-wide accountability performance assessments.

Problem-solving requires a learner to combine previously learned information (declarative knowledge, principles, and strategies) in such a way as to solve a previously unencountered problem. Problem-solving requires an active, deliberate process, rather than a rote response. Therefore, problem-solving is highly dependent on executive processes. Furthermore, because students do not automatically develop problem-solving strategies, these skills must be taught.

To solve problems, students need both *specific* and *general* problem-solving skills. Specific problem-solving skills are useful only in the domain to which they apply, while general problem-solving skills can be used to solve a wide range of problems. For example, to solve a geometry problem, a student would need to have specific declarative knowledge (such as $a^2+b^2=c^2$ where a and b are legs of a right triangle and c is the hypotenuse) and procedural knowledge ("get all the unknowns to one side of the equal sign"). However, a student who knows how to solve a geometry problem would not necessarily also know how to solve geography problems involving population density or cultural diffusion.

General problem-solving involves a set of principles or steps that usually lead to success, regardless of the context. Usually, these steps prompt the learner to (a) identify and define the goal, (b) identify a range of possible strategies for reaching the goal, (c) select the strategy most likely to succeed and devise a plan, (d) carry out the plan, and (e) evaluate the effects of the plan to see if the goal has been met. General problem-solving strategies are less powerful that domain-specific problem-solving. However, because they are not dependent on specific declarative or procedural knowledge, they are useful for students who lack prior knowledge or whose long-term memory is poorly organized.

A number of general problem-solving strategies can help such students. For example, students who consistently rely on a small number of solution strategies can be taught to use brainstorming to generate a larger

Box 3.2   Six-Step Process for Teaching Strategies

To teach strategies, Harris and Graham (1996) suggest a six-stage instructional process:

1. The teacher develops or activates relevant background knowledge, such as the key vocabulary associated with the strategy.

2. The teacher and student discuss the strategy to establish a purpose for using it and identify expected outcomes.

3. Model the strategy, using "think-aloud" or self-instruction techniques.

4. Help the student memorize the steps in the strategy, often using mnemonic devices.

5. Support the student's use of the strategy by providing motivational and corrective feedback.

6. Monitor the student's independent use of the strategy.

set of possible ways to solve a problem. Similarly, students who have difficulty breaking problems down into manageable steps can be taught to use a *means-ends analysis* in which they continually compare their present situation with the desired goal and formulate the "next step." The six-step instructional process for teaching strategies suggested by Harris and Graham (1996) in Box 3.2 can also be used for teaching general problem-solving strategies.

Transfer and Generalization

Researchers who have studied learning have long been interested in how what is learned in one situation can transfer or be applied in another. Much of the early research in this area stressed drill and practice to develop competence in the specific skill areas and the importance of maintaining similarity in skills and facts across settings (Thorndike, 1913). New research recognizes the importance of developing the initial competence in a topic or subject matter, but it also stresses the need to ensure that learning is not overly bound to one setting or type of task and that transfer is always dependent on previous experiences and prior knowledge.

How a student learns new material greatly influences this ability to transfer that knowledge to other settings (Bransford, Brown, and Cocking, 1999). For example, learning that stresses *understanding*, as opposed to rote memorization of facts or procedures, is more likely to transfer to other situations or problems. However, a person could demonstrate complete understanding in one context (that is, have a knowledge base that consists of rich, interconnected networks of facts, concepts, and principles and that can be operated upon in a variety of ways) and incomplete understanding in another (in other words, know a few rules, but not know why or when to apply them). Therefore, one of the most important considerations in helping students transfer learning from one context to another is awareness of the kind of transfer expected.

One distinction that is commonly made is between *near* and *far* transfers. In a near-transfer task, there is much overlap between the situation in which a skill is learned and the situation in which it is later used. An end-of-the-week test in multiplication that presents problems in exactly the same format they were learned in would be an example of a near-transfer task. Far transfer is required when there is little overlap between the original learning situation and the context in which the skill is required. Using the Pythagorean theorem to plan a flower bed after learning to solve geometry problems in the classroom would be an example of a far-transfer task.

It is also important to understand transfer when prior knowledge gets in the way of new learning. For example, irregularities in basic letter/sound relationships can cause a beginning reader many difficulties in initial decoding, or when learning Spanish, a student might employ familiar English pronunciations. Teachers can correct some of the more common ways in which a student can be tripped up by prior knowledge through the use of questioning that requires students to explain why they solved a problem a certain way or gave a specific answer.

Transfer does not occur automatically, but teachers can support it. Here are some classroom strategies to increase transfer:

• **Provide opportunities for students to practice skills and apply knowledge in a variety of contexts.** It is important to help students build links in long-term memory that help them perceive the similarities in various situations that would trigger the use of a particular piece of information or procedure to be transferred.

• **Systematically vary types of examples from near to far transfers.** Gradually introduce elements of the transfer situation into the examples students encounter so that the transition from the learned task to the transfer task takes the form of many small near-transfer steps, rather than a single far-transfer leap. You can vary the size of the steps according to the amount of prior knowledge your students can readily activate and the distance of the transfer task from the original learning task. For example, to help students transfer subtraction of three-digit numerals in columnar problems to a two-step word problem involving money, you might systematically introduce the following elements in successive lessons or examples: addition and subtraction problems involving decimals, addition and subtraction involving money labels, one-step word problems involving two-digit and three-digit subtraction, two-step word problems involving subtraction with decimals, and finally two-step word problems involving two-digit subtraction with money labels.

- **Model strategies that show how previously learned information can be used in a new situation.** Teachers can use think-aloud procedures or other ways to make covert thought processes observable for students. For example, while demonstrating how to conduct an Internet or library search, a teacher might model a set of problem-solving self-questions taught during a math class: What is my goal? What do I know already? What do I need to find out? What steps do I need to follow to reach my goal? Have I reached my goal yet?

- **Provide cues in situations where students are required to transfer previously learned information.** For example, you might prompt students' use of a prewriting strategy learned in the context of narrative story writing when they are writing a letter with a statement such as this one: "You can plan your letter using brainstorming the same way you did when you made up the stories we wrote last week. Who remembers how to use brainstorming?"

The Learning-Teaching Connection

Instruction must be designed on the basis of what it is students will be expected to learn. The nature of the information shapes the instruction. However, humans use different cognitive processes to learn different types of information, so it is only through careful consideration of both the information and the thinking processes required for learning the information that an effective learning-teaching connection can be made. Here are the major points we discussed in this chapter:

- As a stimulus (or information) from the environment is detected through one of the senses, it is held briefly in sensory memory until it can be analyzed. The primary functions here are attention and recognition. Because sensory memory has an extremely limited capacity, effective teachers use a variety of strategies to focus and maintain student attention and aid in recognition. These strategies include signals to indicate the beginning and end of activities; movements, gestures, and speech patterns that maintain attention; variations in materials and activities; and a variety of types of questions to aid recognition.

- Information is held in working memory temporarily while it is compared with information already stored in long-term memory. Working memory also has a limited capacity, but it is possible to retain information there for longer periods of time through rehearsal and by chunking smaller bits of information into larger units.

- Encoding new information in long-term memory is probably the most important component of the learning process. Information that has been encoded effectively is more likely to be retrieved than information that is not stored properly.

* The more often information is encountered, the more likely it is to be easily retrieved when needed. This is why it is important for teachers to provide opportunities for their students to practice using recently learned information. Distributed practice is much more effective than massed practice because it increases the frequency with which a learner encounters the to-be-learned information and activates relevant prior knowledge in long-term memory.

* When a student lacks sufficient prior knowledge to make a connection with new information being taught, the teacher must provide temporary supports, often called *scaffolding,* to augment the student's existing knowledge.

* Learners develop structures and schemes for organizing information in long-term memory. These structures govern comprehension as well as how efficiently the learner uses what they already know. Learning failures can occur if the learner's long-term memory is poorly organized.

* Learners who have a large, well-organized, readily accessible store of prior knowledge in long-term memory are better able to process information through working memory than those who lack prior knowledge or are less able to access information stored in long-term memory.

* Problem-solving requires a learner to combine previously learned information in such a way as to solve a previously unencountered problem. Problem-solving is highly dependent on executive processes, and because students do not automatically develop problem-solving strategies, these skills must be taught.

* To solve problems, students need both *specific* and *general* problem-solving skills. Specific problem-solving skills are useful only in the domain to which they apply, while general problem-solving skills can be used to solve a wide range of problems. General problem-solving involves a set of principles or steps that usually lead to success, regardless of the context.

* How a student learns new material greatly influences this ability to transfer that knowledge to other settings. A person could demonstrate complete understanding in one context and incomplete understanding in another. Therefore, it is important to provide opportunities for students to practice skills and apply knowledge in a variety of contexts and to discriminate the characteristics of different situations that require information learned previously in a different context.

4

EVALUATING THE OUTCOMES OF ACCESS

Special educators sometimes seem to have a preoccupation with assessment and evaluation. The roots of this tradition probably can be found in the medical model that dominated special education until very recently. It was often believed that a student's unique learning problems could be "diagnosed" and a specialized "treatment" plan could be developed to remediate their problems. As we discussed in the first chapter, this traditional diagnostic-treatment model of special education often led to the development of educational goals that focused on isolated skills that had little connection to larger curriculum outcomes.

In this book, we have been talking about a new model of special education, articulated in the Individuals with Disabilities Education Act of 1997 (IDEA-97), in which a student's Individualized Education Plan (IEP) focuses on the accommodations and modifications needed to help the student succeed in the general curriculum. It is no longer enough for a school to assert that a student has access to the general curriculum simply because they are placed in a general education classroom or because they receive instruction in general education curriculum materials. It is now assumed that a student who does not make meaningful *progress* toward general curriculum goals has not had adequate access to the general curriculum.

This higher standard, *progress in the general curriculum*, requires educators to use a new set of assessment and measurement tools and to think differently about the role of assessment in instruction. In this chapter, we will explore the problem-solving needed to evaluate whether a student is making progress in the general curriculum. We will do this by looking at the yardsticks educators use to make decisions about student performance.

Assessment and Decision-Making

All educational assessment is aimed at answering questions. Sometimes the question is as straightforward as, "Should this student move on to the next level of the reading curriculum?" or "Have my students learned the most important concepts related to electromagnetism?" At other times, the question is much more complex, such as, "Does this student have a learning disability?" or "Is this an effective school?" Regardless of the complexity of the question, though, the decisions educators seek to make with assessments usually involve the comparison of student performance with a standard. A standard is simply a known unit to which the thing being measured can be compared or "referenced." A tape measure used to measure a piece of lumber is a standard, as is a measuring cup used to measure ingredients in a recipe.

In education, three standards commonly are used. These are norm-referencing, criteria-referencing, and individual-referencing. Norm-referencing involves the comparison of an individual's performance with that of a particular group. Criterion-referencing entails comparison of an individual's performance with an objective or with a performance standard, such as a scoring rubric or rating scale. Individual-referencing involves the comparison of a student's performance on a task at one point in time with their previous performance on the same task. These three reference standards are compared in Figure 4.1 and are discussed in the sections that follow.

Norm-Referenced Decisions

Norm-referenced assessment tools are useful whenever it is important to know how a particular student or group of students compares with a reference or "norm" group. Norm-referencing enables an evaluator to make a judgment about whether a particular student is "different." The further an individual's scores fall from average, which is usually the mean of the norm group, the more different the individual is considered to be.

Figure 4.1   Reference standards

Comparison Point	Norm-Referenced	Criterion-Referenced	Individual-Referenced
Principle use	Screening and eligibility testing	Mastery testing	Monitor progress toward long-range goals
Major emphasis	Measure inter-individual differences in achievements	Describe tasks a student can perform in a particular domain	Measure individual growth over time
Interpretation of results	Compare performance to that of other individuals	Compare performance to a clearly defined domain that may be contained in curriculum standards	Compare the actual rate of progress to the expected or desired rate
Content coverage	Covers a broad area of achievement	Focuses on a particular set of learning tasks	Items sampled from within the curriculum but across instructional units (such as "20 passages from level 4.2 of the basal reading series")
Performance standards	The level of performance is determined by a relative position in some known group ("ranks fifth in group of 20")	The level of performance is determined by absolute standards ("has accurately completed 90% of all objectives") or scoring rubric ("scored four on a five-point scale")	The rate of change is calculated and compared to the expected or desired growth

Source: Adapted from Tindal and Marston, 1990

Most published norm-referenced tests are "normed" on a large sample of subjects who take various versions of the test while it is being developed. Test items are modified, added, and deleted during this development process until the distribution of scores obtained by the norm group takes the form of a *normal distribution*. This is the familiar shape commonly referred to as a bell curve. Because norm-referencing requires standardized administration and scoring procedures to ensure that everyone who takes the test does so under the same conditions, these tests are commonly referred to as *standardized tests*.

The statistical properties of normal distributions are what make possible the kind of norm-referenced decision-making with which most educators are familiar. All normal distributions are symmetrical, with approximately 68 percent of the cases falling within plus or minus one standard deviation of the mean and approximately 96 percent of the cases falling within plus or minus two standard deviations of the mean. A score that is one standard deviation below the mean is lower than about 84 percent of the people in the norm group who took the test. For example, if a person obtains a score of 70 on a norm-referenced intelligence test that has a mean of 100 and a standard deviation of 15, only about 16 percent of the people who take the test would be likely to get a lower score. Many educators would consider this performance different enough to make the individual eligible for special education.

Standardized tests such as the Iowa Test of Basic Skills (Hoover, Hieronymus, Frisbie, and Dunbar, 1993) or the California Achievement Test (CTB-McGraw-Hill, 1985) frequently are used to evaluate school performance. This is accomplished by comparing scores of the students in a school with those of the national norm group. However, these tests are not linked to a particular set of outcomes or standards, nor are they based on any particular curriculum materials. Therefore, it is possible for all of the students in a school to score above the mean of their respective norm groups but still not make progress toward local curriculum goals.

Norm-referencing is limited in its utility for making judgments about a student's progress in the general curriculum. Norm-referencing cannot provide useful information about a student's present level of performance in a particular skill or content area, nor can norm-referenced assessment help a teacher decide what a student needs to learn next. Questions of this type can only be answered with criterion-referenced measures.

Criterion-Referenced Decisions

A criterion-referenced evaluation involves comparing the performance of an individual with the characteristics of a particular domain. The early use of criterion-referenced testing often involved lists of objectives thought to represent competent performance in a particular skill or content area. A set of test items was developed to test each objective, and the more items a student "passed," the more of the domain they were thought to have "mastered." Usually, pass/no pass criteria were established on the basis of the expert judgment of the test developer or through some normative process.

The school accountability measures in wide use today are a variation on the theme of criterion-referenced testing. Only now domains such as "reading," "writing," and "social studies" are represented by curriculum standards, benchmarks, and indicators, rather than discrete instructional objectives. Schools are evaluated on the basis of the number of students who successfully "master" the various curriculum standards measured on the tests. Some states establish specific targets linked to incentives or sanctions. For example, schools may be expected to show that at least 70 percent of their students obtain scores of at least three on a five-point scale.

The most innovative aspect of this updated use of criterion-referenced assessments is the tests themselves. Often referred to as *alternative assessments* because they are viewed as alternatives to standardized tests, these measures require students to actively perform tasks or create products. Frequently, these tasks are intended to reflect "real-world" or *authentic* contexts as a direct measure of learning. Lately, the term *performance assessment* has gained general acceptance in the professional literature to refer to the entire class of extended response measures being used in school accountability testing.

In its purest form, performance assessment involves a judge observing and subjectively evaluating an individual who actually is carrying out an activity. Performance assessments have been used for years in athletic competitions such as gymnastics or figure skating as well as in the performing arts. Anyone who has ever watched the Olympics is familiar with this assessment strategy. In classrooms, where learning and thinking are largely covert or "inside the head" activities, a performance assessment often focuses on products rather than activities. For example, students may build a model structure, such as a bridge or tower, and then write an explanation of the calculations and steps involved. Such products are intended to tap multiple skills across disciplines. It is assumed that the quality of the product is a reflection of the quality of the thinking that underlies it.

Performance assessment takes some getting used to. Students accustomed to selection-response, norm-referenced tests, and traditional, teacher-made tests often have difficulty with tasks that require multiple steps and extended responses that integrate knowledge across skill domains. However, as many teachers have discovered in the last few years, simply teaching students how to take the test will have only a minimal impact on student performance. To be successful on these tests, students must learn to integrate and use knowledge and strategies accrued over an extended period of time.

The unapologetic expectation of policy makers who mandate performance assessments is that the curriculum and instruction to which students are exposed will change to reflect the standards upon which the assessment program is based. In this respect, the assessment process is explicitly intended to bring about fundamental changes in classroom practices. This dimension of an assessment has been termed *systemic validity* (Fredericksen & Collins, 1989).

Systemic Validity

According to Fredericksen and Collins (1989), a systematically valid test is one that changes the instructional system to foster the development of the *cognitive skills* a test is designed to measure. When an assessment program is systematically valid, instruction focuses on the cognitive processes involved in performing the assessment tasks, rather than on completing specific examples of the task. This could be thought of as teaching to the process, rather than teaching to the test. Using systematically valid, criterion-referenced assessments requires teachers to think differently about how and what they teach. Students must be taught how to *use* information, rather than just acquire it. An example of the change in thinking that many teachers must undergo is provided in Box 4.1.

A systemically valid assessment has two key attributes. First, it employs direct measures of the cognitive skills being tested and, second, it employs subjective or qualitative scoring systems.

Direct Measurement

The distinction between direct and indirect tasks may be difficult to grasp at first, but the distinction is an important one when we consider the kind of thinking and problem-solving implied by the curriculum frameworks. Direct measures are those that enable the observation of the thinking or problem-solving a student is expected to learn. Indirect measures are those that require the teacher to make an inference about the student's ability to use the thinking or problem-solving process they are expected to have learned.

Recall that throughout this book we have discussed the various types of information that are contained in the general curriculum (facts, concepts, principles, procedures, and strategies). We showed the distinctions

Box 4.1   Teaching to the Process

Ms. Wolf is a seventh-grade social studies teacher. She uses the *Social Studies for Today* curriculum series. This series provides the teacher with ready-made lecture outlines, homework assignments, and end-of-unit tests. Ms. Wolf likes using in-class simulation activities that she makes up because they give students lots of opportunities to use the concepts that she feels are important. However, she is disappointed that her students find the activities so difficult. Students always ask her for the correct answer and seem unable to handle the idea that more than one correct answer might make sense in some situations. Her students seem to be good at answering the items on the end-of-unit tests, but they seem unable to use the information contained in the chapter to solve "real-life" problems. Ms. Wolf also finds that if she strays too far from the lecture notes provided by the curriculum program, students tend to do poorly on the end-of-unit tests.

Ms. Wolf began to suspect that the end-of-unit tests do not representatively sample the domain in which she provides instruction. When she looks closer, she realizes the tests require mostly reiterations of facts. She knows she could get her students to score high on these tests just by going over the specific facts included on the test. Ms. Wolf decides to make up her own performance assessments that require students to evaluate, predict, and apply key concepts and principles. She finds that students don't know where to begin. When asked to think critically, the students often do not provide a rationale for the decision they make. In making a prediction, students tend to summarize the information in the prompt but don't move beyond this information to tell what will happen next. Or when they make predications, often these are based on conjecture, rather than on key concepts and principles.

Ms. Wolf begins to teach her students some strategies for making evaluations, predictions, and applications. She shows the students that to make an evaluation they need to indicate a clear choice among the options presented and then present a convincing argument for making the choice. She teaches the students the difference between this and simply summarizing information given in the prompt.

Similarly, she shows her students that in making predictions, they need to provide a cogent rationale for making a highly probable prediction, rather than making a guess based on opinion. Finally, Ms. Wolf shows her students how to use the skills in a wide range of social studies contexts. Each new chapter in the textbook presents a new context in which to teach her students to use complex intellectual operations. Soon the students begin obtaining higher scores on the performance assessments that Ms. Wolf makes for each unit.

among facts, concepts, principles, and procedures in Figure 2.2. The format of the information contained in the curriculum determines the kind of thinking a student would use. The more complex the information, the more useful it is for higher order thinking and problem-solving. Simple information such as facts and concrete concepts can only be used in simple thinking processes such as verbatim reiteration. The various cognitive operations that can be performed with facts, concepts, and principles are shown in Figure 4.2. This table is based on a taxonomy developed by Williams and Haladyna (1978) as well as the classic work of Bloom and colleagues (1958).

Direct measures of higher order thinking are those that require students to solve problems using evaluation, prediction, and the application of concepts and principles. Indirect measures are those that simply require students to summarize and reiterate facts, concepts, and principles but never use them to solve complex problems in a performance assessment. The example from science in Box 4.2 illustrates this distinction.

The first three items, which require reiteration or summarization, are indirect tasks of thinking because students are never asked to demonstrate an understanding of the effects of human behavior on salmon habitats, the stated goals of instruction. They simply need to recall declarative information stored in long-term memory and produce it in the same format in which it was learned. The last item, which requires students to use information more actively, is a direct measure of students' use of the cognitive task of *application*, described in Figure 4.2. In application, the student is presented with a current situation and explains the circumstances that most likely occurred to bring it about. To respond to this item, students need to use declarative information (the lifecycle of salmon and the effects of human behavior) as well as conditional knowledge, the principle "the more development that occurs along streams, the less healthy the salmon population"). Any of the three choices could be correct and each could be supported with information that was provided during instruction. However, a student's presentation of a rationale for a particular choice would provide a more direct measure of their thinking and understanding.

The first three items would be scored as either right or wrong, but the last item would be judged on a continuum, or *scale* of competence, based on the accuracy of the information as well as the strength of the argument used. Scaling implies that thinking and understanding can exist to varying degrees, rather than in a can/can't dichotomy. All students would be assumed to be able to engage in some level of complex thinking about salmon habitats, but some would have a more complete understanding and be able to use that knowledge more effectively.

An assessment that permits locating student performance on a continuum is extremely useful for monitoring student progress in the larger content domains associated with curriculum standards and, as we will discuss in the next chapter, the development of meaningful IEPs that index the general curriculum. This assessment strategy is based on the

Figure 4.2 Cognitive operations for three kinds of information

Cognitive Operation	Facts	Concepts	Principles
Reiterate	Verbatim reproduction of the information presented during instruction. *Example:* "Albany is the capital of New York."	Verbatim reproduction of the concept name and defining attributes. *Example:* "A triangle is a three-sided polygon."	Verbatim reproduction of the rule. *Example:* "If you heat a gas, it will expand."
Summarize	Reproduce the fact in a slightly different form. *Example:* "The capital of New York is Albany."	Reproduce the concept name and defining attributes in a different form. *Example:* "A shape that has only three sides is a triangle."	Reproduce the rule in a different form. *Example:* "Heating a gas will cause it to expand."
Illustrate	Can't be done.	Recognize or generate an example not previously encountered. *Example:* Student draws a triangle when asked to do so.	Provide or recognize an example that shows the relationship stated in the rule. *Example:* Student observes balloon burst when held over candle and then states the rule.
Predict	Can't be done.	Tell what will happen in another setting or at some point in the future. Can only be done with some concepts. *Example:* Teacher removes one side of a square made of sticks and asks the student to tell what will be created if the remaining sticks are joined. Student replies "triangle."	Tell what will happen, given the first part of the rule. *Example:* Teacher: "What do you think will happen if we hold this bottle over the burner?" Student: "The air inside will expand and make the cork fly off."
Evaluate	Can't be done.	Make a choice or decision and provide a rationale. Can only be done with some concepts. *Example:* Teacher: "Which of these is a better example of a triangle?" Student: "This one, it has three sides that are all connected."	Make a choice or decision and provide a rationale. *Example:* Teacher: "Which situation best shows the rule?" Student: "This one, the gas only expanded after it was heated. In the other one, expansion was caused by a chemical reaction, not heat."
Apply	Can't be done.	Given a situation, tell what circumstances created it. Can only be done with some concepts. *Example:* Teacher: "How did we end up with a triangle?" Student: "First, you took one side off of the square and then you joined the other three sides."	Given a situation, tell what circumstances created it. *Example:* Teacher: "Why did the tire burst when the bike was left in the sun?" Student: "The air inside the tire got warm and expanded."

Box 4.2   Examples of Direct and Indirect Measures

One of the benchmarks for a science standard in a particular state curriculum framework is that students will understand how interactions among systems can cause changes in matter and energy. An indicator for this benchmark is that a student will be able to explain how the human use of natural resources affects the health of ecosystems. In a recent unit on endangered species in a middle school classroom, much classroom discussion was devoted to salmon restoration. The goal of instruction was for students to identify human behaviors that affect salmon habitats. Equal amounts of time were spent on the salmon lifecycle, the habitats in which salmon live at different phases of their lives, and human behaviors that affect salmon habitats.

The teacher now wants to make up a test that will measure students' mastery of the benchmark and indicator. Here is one set of questions a teacher could ask:

1. Name three phases of the lifecycle of the chinook salmon:

2. Which of the following is not a habitat in which salmon live at some point in their lives?
   (a) deep ocean (b) estuary (c) warm pond (d) cool stream

3. What is runoff?

Here is another item that would test the same content:

Imagine you are living in the year 2070. Your favorite thing to do is to go fishing and your favorite fish to catch is the coho salmon, a species that is native to your area. Coho are abundant in the streams in your area, along with many other species of fish, such as steelhead, rainbow trout, and chinook salmon. You know that back in the year 2000, salmon were on the endangered species list, but today they are thriving. Which of the following situations do you suppose *most* contributed to the health of native salmon in the year 2070?

a) Many salmon hatcheries were developed and farm-raised salmon were released at sea.

b) Strict limits were placed on agricultural, commercial, and industrial development along streams where salmon breed.

c) Genetic engineering led to the development of more disease-resistant salmon.

Write a short essay that explains your answer.

---

idea that all students can move along a continuum of competence, regardless of their beginning level performance. In other words, all students can make meaningful progress in the general curriculum. Of course, this approach requires a strategy for assigning values to different levels of performance along that continuum, which brings us to the second important attribute of a systematically valid assessment: the use of subjective scoring procedures.

Subjective Scoring

Subjective scoring involves the application of expert knowledge to judge the adequacy of a student response. With subjective scoring, no single correct answer exists. Student performance is judged according to a set of criteria pertaining to the levels of proficiency. Usually, this judgment is made with the help of scoring rubrics.

A *rubric* is a set of scoring guidelines that describes a range of possible responses for a particular assessment item. Generally, a rubric contains a scale that indicates the points that will be assigned to a student's work and a set of descriptors for each point on that scale. Scales of three-, four-, or five-points are commonly used in schools, with the highest value on the scale representing the most proficient performance.

Two general categories of rubrics exist: holistic and analytic. With holistic scoring, a quick overall impression of a student's work is formed and then compared with exemplars or "range finders" that represent various levels of competence.

Holistic rubrics can be developed quickly and provide information about the range of performance within a particular group of students (see Box 4.3). However, holistic rubrics do not necessarily provide information about student performance relative to specific curriculum outcomes. Work samples are rated only in comparison with all other samples in the group, so it is possible that even the best sample in the group may not be particularly good when compared with an external standard. This is why analytic rubrics are a more useful tool for making criterion-referenced decisions about student performance.

Analytic rubrics provide a set of predetermined statements that clearly describes the performance corresponding to each point on the scale. These statements are established before student work is evaluated and are intended to describe clearly the continuum of competence along which a learner would move to become more proficient. An example of an analytic scoring rubric for evaluating persuasive essays is shown in Figure 4.3, and Figure 4.4 shows a set of rubrics for evaluating mathematics problem-solving.

Well-designed analytic rubrics can provide clear criteria for evaluating student performance when they are tied directly to curriculum outcomes (Thorndike, 1997). Here are some general characteristics of well-designed scoring rubrics:

Box 4.3   Procedures for Creating Holistic Scoring Rubrics

Here are the general procedures that Tindal and Marston (1990) suggest for developing holistic scoring rubrics:

1. Quickly review all of the samples of work in the group and identify one or two range finders corresponding to each point on the scale you want to develop. For example, if you want a four-point scale, you might identify eight exemplars.

2. Examine the range finders and decide which characteristics of the work make it an example of the scale value it is intended to represent. For example, if you are evaluating writing samples, decide what characteristics the "4" papers have in common that make them a "4" and what distinguishes the "3" papers from the "2" papers, and so on.

3. Develop a summary description of the attributes that distinguish each anchor point on the scale.

4. Examine the remainder of the work samples in the group and compare them with the range finders and the summary descriptions of each scale value. Assign each of the remaining work samples a score, based on the range finder it most closely resembles.

Figure 4.3   Rubric for scoring persuasive-essays

Score	Interpretation
5	The writer identifies a clear position and fully supports it with solid evidence that includes personal and or factual information: • The arguments are logical. • The arguments are backed by fact/experience.
4	The writer identifies a clear position but fails to support it *fully* with solid evidence that includes personal and or factual information: • The arguments may be *slightly* flawed. • The arguments may be weakly backed by fact/experience.
3	The writer identifies a clear position, but the position lacks clarity. It is unclear what the writer is trying to say: • The arguments may be present but illogical. • The arguments are not backed by fact/experience. • The reliance is on emotion, not the topic.
2	The writer's position is not clearly articulated and can only be inferred. The writer may offer contradictory opinions or positions: • The arguments are weak or irrelevant. • The arguments are not backed by fact/experience. • The reliance is on emotion, not the topic.
1	The writer presents a vague or ambiguous position that can only be inferred. Supporting arguments may be offered, but they are illogical or irrelevant.
0	No response or response is unacceptable.

- Rubrics used to monitor progress in the general curriculum should be linked directly to clearly stated curriculum standards. Effective rubrics often include related benchmarks or indicators as part of the rubric.

- Well-defined rubrics use descriptive language that focuses on the key feature of the performance being considered. It should be readily apparent in the rubric what dimension of performance is being evaluated.

- Effective rubrics clearly indicate a continuum of proficiency ranging from novice to expert. There should be a direct relationship among descriptors at various points on the scale.

- A single rubric should focus on only one dimension of performance. When more than one dimension is important, separate rubrics should be

EVALUATING THE OUTCOMES OF ACCESS

Figure 4.4   Math problem-solving rubric

Score	Interpretation
4	• The student uses effective problem-solving strategies and demonstrates a complete understanding of the dimensions of the problem. • No inaccuracies or computation errors are evident. • Data are well organized and displayed effectively. • All conclusions are based on data and logically supported with pertinent details.
3	• The student demonstrates a reasonable understanding of the problem and generally uses effective problem-solving strategies. • Some minor errors or inaccuracies are present, but they do not affect the solution or conclusion. • Data generally are well organized and for the most part are displayed effectively. • Conclusions are generally supported by data and are logical
2	• The student demonstrates an incomplete grasp of the problem but does attempt to use a problem-solving strategy. • The problem contains substantial errors or inaccuracies that interfere with the solution. • Data are ineffectively organized or displayed. • Conclusions do not follow from data or are illogical.
1	• The student demonstrates a minimal understanding of the problem or uses an ineffective problem-solving strategy. • Major errors or inaccuracies are present and interfere with the solution. • Data are poorly organized or displayed, or may not be displayed at all. • Conclusions are illogical or irrelevant.
0	No response or response is unacceptable.

used for each. For example, a separate rubric pertaining to "organization and cohesion" could also be used to the persuasiveness writing scale, shown in Figure 4.3. Similarly, a separate rubric would be needed to scale "communicating about math problem-solving" because communication skills are not addressed in the rubric in Figure 4.4.

• Well-designed rubrics include enough scale points to enable meaningful discrimination among levels of proficiency but not so many as to make scoring unreliable. Generally, rubrics should contain no fewer than three points and no more than seven points. A "zero" point should be included to differentiate "no performance" from very novice performance.

• Effective rubrics focus on the outcome of performance, rather than the process a student uses. The emphasis should be on the evidence of proficiency, rather than the effort expended. For example, it usually is not very useful to design rubrics to scale student effort or the extent to which a student enjoys or appreciates an activity. Although these may be instructionally relevant variables, they may not be valid indicators of performance.

* Rubrics should be shared with the student while they are in the process of learning the skills or knowledge that will later be evaluated with the rubric. This strategy clearly communicates what the student will be expected to do to demonstrate proficiency and what dimensions of performance the teacher values. Rubric descriptors should be easily interpreted and meaningful to the student.

Scoring rubrics lend themselves very well to describing a student's present level of performance relative to a curriculum outcome. However, the points on a rubric only represent mileposts along a continuum of competence; rubrics are not equal interval scales. The difference between a performance that scores a "1" and one that scores a "2" may be much greater than the difference between "4" and "5" performances. Also, rubrics may not be very sensitive to growth that occurs in less than four to six months if they are intended to reference larger curriculum outcomes, rather than short-term instruction. For these reasons, even under optimal instructional conditions, it may take a student months to move up a single point on a rubric scale. Of course, if the instruction to which a student is being exposed is not effective, it will take even longer. In any case, it would take a teacher who is using only rubrics to measure growth an unacceptably long time to discover that a student is not progressing in the general curriculum. This is the main reason we suggest that criterion-referenced performance assessments should be used in conjunction with individual-referenced evaluation.

Individual Referenced Decision-Making

Individual referenced decision-making involves systematic comparisons of a student's current work with their previous performance. Individual referenced evaluation often is referred to as *formative evaluation*, because the effects of instruction are evaluated on an ongoing basis, rather than after all instruction has been delivered. Instruction is modified whenever the evaluation indicates that students are not learning.

Individual-referenced evaluation has often been used to monitor progress toward special education IEP goals using procedures associated with *curriculum-based measurement* (CBM) (Deno, 1985). CBM was originally developed by Stanley Deno and associates at the University of Minnesota Institute for Research on Learning Disabilities. In the last 15 years, CBM has been researched extensively and found to be a technically adequate means for making data-based decisions about student learning, primarily in the basic skills of reading, written expression, math computation, and spelling. With CBM, students respond directly on brief "probes" that are sampled from the curriculum materials in use in their local classroom or school. The administration and scoring of CBM probes is standardized and the unit for summarizing student performance is fluency, rather than just accuracy.

Deno's original idea in developing CBM was for teachers to have a quick measure of students' academic "vital signs," analogous to the measures of pulse, temperature, and blood pressure that medical practitioners use to monitor a person's physical health. In reading, students read orally for one minute. In written expression, students write narrative essays for three to five minutes in response to story starters. In spelling, students write 10 to 15 words presented in rolling dictation. In math computation, students complete basic skills probes (addition, subtraction, multiplication, and division) for three to five minutes. At the secondary level, CBM has involved maze and vocabulary matching tasks sampled from content curriculum materials (Espin and Tindal, 1998). These measures use objective scoring procedures, rather than the subjective rating scales we discussed in the last section. For example, reading might be scored as the total number of words read correctly in one minute, math as the total number of correct digits supplied, and written expression as the percent of correctly spelled words or correct word sequences.

These measures are intended to provide a "quick and dirty" look at a student's educational performance, rather than the more extensive information about thinking and learning processes that would be evaluated with a performance assessment. As with their medical analogs, if a student's vital signs are acceptable, no further assessment would be merited. However, if these quick checks indicate a student is having difficulty, a more extensive evaluation would be undertaken.

Teachers usually make this quick assessment through a visual analysis of data or with the help of a computer program (Fuchs, 1998). A probe is administered each week and the score is plotted on a graph such as the one shown in Figure 4.5.

This graph shows the percent of words spelled correctly on a five-minute writing probe administered once each week. In week 1, the student spelled about 20 percent of the words on the essay correctly. By week 9, the student spelled about 35 percent of the words on the probe correctly. The dashed line is an *aimline* representing the long-term goal for the student. If this graph were drawn to show the entire school year, the aimline would show the slope of progress the student would need to make to move from her or his level of performance at the beginning of the year to the level of performance indicated in her or his annual goal. In this case, the long-term goal is for the student to spell 100 percent of the words on the writing probe correctly.

Aimlines assist in the development of *decision rules* to evaluate the effectiveness of instruction. Here is a typical decision rule: "Whenever progress is

Figure 4.5   Individual-referenced data -

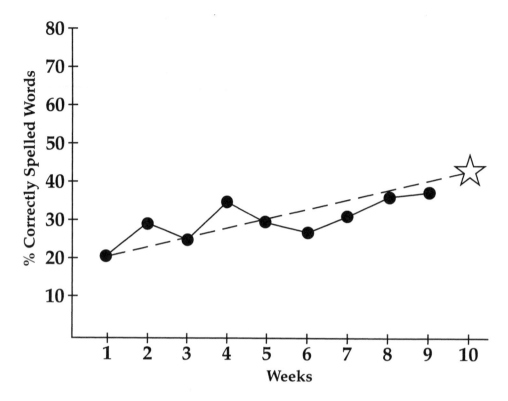

below the aimline for three consecutive data points, a change of instruction is indicated; whenever the student's progress is above the aimline for three consecutive data points, a more ambitious goal is developed." According to this decision rule, the data illustrated in Figure 4.5 indicate that a change in instruction is needed. Even though the student has made steady progress, his or her performance has been below the aimline for four consecutive weeks. If this rate of growth is projected out for the entire school year, the student will not achieve the annual goal of spelling 100 percent of the words correctly on the five-minute writing probe. If the student's performance was above the aimline for the last three or four weeks, the teacher would write a new goal (such as "all words spelled correctly and no more than three errors of punctuation or capitalization on the five-minute writing task").

An individual-referenced evaluation generally focuses on subcomponents or the prerequisite skills of larger curriculum goals and benchmarks. For example, math problem-solving, as described in the rubric shown in Figure 4.4, requires accurate computation. If computation errors consistently contribute to a student's poor performance on math problem-solving, a teacher may choose to monitor this single dimension of a student's performance with weekly math computation probes. Similarly, a teacher may choose to monitor a student's reading proficiency (clearly a preskill needed for most complex performance tasks) using weekly oral reading fluency probes. If it is clear from an individual-referenced evaluation that a student is not making sufficient growth in computation or reading fluency, a teacher would make an instructional change.

However, it is critical to remember that the goal is not to increase a student's basic skills simply for the sake of improving basic skills. The goal always is to help the student make progress in the general curriculum. In other words, just because you are monitoring progress in oral reading fluency doesn't necessarily mean you need to devote a lot of instructional time to teaching students to "read faster." This would be equivalent to sucking on an ice cube just before you have your temperature taken. The only reason to focus instructional time on reading fluency is if the problems a student experiences are fluency-based. Otherwise, concentrate your instructional resources on helping the student become better at the general outcome of reading as it pertains to general curriculum goals. This might involve teaching decoding skills, comprehension strategies, vocabulary, an awareness of genres, or any of the wide range of variables related to reading.

Here are the general procedures for using individual-referenced evaluations:

1. Identify the general outcome you want to measure. These are subcomponents of larger curriculum goals. Examples include written expressions, math problem-solving, reading decoding or fluency for beginning readers, and reading comprehension for older readers. Often the scope and sequence of curriculum materials can help guide this process.

2. Identify tasks that are key indicators of the general outcome. An indicator is not the general outcome expected; it is just a correlate. For example, oral reading fluency is correlated with other measures of reading such as comprehension and teacher ratings. Similarly, computation might be an indicator of math problem-solving. Short narrative essays might be an indicator of more general writing proficiency.

3. Find out the student's present level of performance on the task you have chosen as an indicator of the general outcome. This step usually involves the administration of one or more direct measures of the task. For example, you might find out a student's present level of performance in math computation by administering a series of two-minute addition, subtraction, multiplication, or division probes.

4. Identify a long-term goal for the outcome you want to measure. Goals can be established normatively or through expert judgment. Local norms can be established with a small group of "typical students" at a grade level. For example, to find out what constitutes a "typical" reading for the fourth grade in a school, you could ask the eight students in the middle reading group to read aloud for one minute from a passage they should be able to

read fluently by late January (or roughly the middle of the school year). It is possible to develop more precise and elaborate school or district norms using CBM, but the investment of resources necessary for this effort probably is not merited by the increase in precision that would be gained. When a student is performing below the grade level of her or his peers, local norms should be developed across grade levels to establish useful goals.

5. Develop alternate forms of probes for the task to be measured. These probes must sample the goal material. For example, if the long-term goal for a student who currently is only 20 percent accurate in solving two- and three-digit subtraction problems is to solve them with 100 percent accuracy, the alternate forms of the probe would consist of two- and three-digit subtraction problems, regardless of the student's present instructional level. The idea is that over time, if instruction is effective, the student will make steady progress toward the goal. If a measurement is conducted using only single-digit subtraction facts, the student would soon "outgrow" the measurement tool. The analogy here is the measuring tape attached to the wall of a child's bedroom. If the tape is only three feet long, the child will eventually outgrow it and a new tape will be needed. The idea in developing probes for an individual-referenced evaluation is to select a long enough tape right from the start.

6. Administer the probes on a weekly basis under standardized conditions. Be sure to use a different probe each week to avoid the effects of practice or memory. It is usually acceptable to use a probe again after about two months. Therefore, 12 to 15 versions usually would be needed for an entire school year. It is critical that each administration of the probe be the same so that meaningful interpretations can be made. Obviously, if a student has three minutes to write one week and 10 minutes the next, it would be difficult to evaluate the meaning of differences in the two writing samples.

7. Plot weekly data on a graph that also includes an aimline. The visual analysis of data typically involves estimating the slope or "trend" of the line of best fit. This is a simple procedure that has been described frequently. For more information about this process, the reader should consult Tindal and Marston (1990) or Howell and Nolet (2000).

8. Evaluate after every five or six data points and apply decision rules. Usually, an instructional change is warranted whenever a student is not making sufficient progress and a more ambitious goal is developed whenever a student exceeds their aimline.

Evaluating Progress in the General Curriculum

Evaluating student progress in the general curriculum involves multiple assessment strategies. No single measure will provide enough information. Therefore, it is important for teachers to see how the various

Figure 4.6 Schedule for using progress monitoring tools

Frequency	Procedure	Purpose
Every two or three years	State-mandated school accountability measures employing performance assessment and scoring rubrics	To evaluate school effectiveness at teaching curriculum standards and benchmarks
Once a year	Published, norm-referenced achievement tests	To compare students in a particular school or classroom with a national norm sample
Three to four times a year	Locally developed (district, school, or teacher) performance assessments linked to curriculum standards and benchmarks using scoring rubrics and monitoring individual student progress	To evaluate students' use of complex thinking and problem-solving contained in curriculum
Once a month	Curriculum-based measures of larger subcomponent skills such as written expression and math problem-solving using objective scoring procedures and decision rules	Monitor progress in skills that are subcomponents of larger curriculum outcomes
Once a week	Curriculum-based measures of basic skills such as oral reading fluency, math computation, or vocabulary using objective scoring procedures and decision rules	To monitor progress in the acquisition of basic skills associated with performance in larger domains

procedures we discussed in this chapter fit together. Here is a summary of the key points we discussed:

- The educational decision you want to make will determine the reference standard you use. Different reference standards require different measurement tools.

- Norm-referenced tools simply tell about relative standing. Is this student different?

- Criterion-referenced tools tell about status in a domain. How much of the curriculum has the student mastered? How well does the student perform?

- Scoring rubrics can clearly describe the continuum of proficiency a student is expected to move along.

- Individual-referenced evaluation tools tell whether a student is making progress toward specific outcomes that are subcomponents of larger curriculum outcomes.

Evaluating progress in the general curriculum requires an integrated evaluation program that combines all of these tools, but they don't all need to be used every day. Remember, never let teaching take a back seat to testing. *When in doubt, teach.* Testing is just a way to see if your teaching has been effective. Figure 4.6 shows a suggested schedule for using the tools we have been discussing to monitor the success of your students in the general curriculum.

5

ACCESS TO CURRICULUM AND THE INDIVIDUAL EDUCATION PROGRAM

The Individual Education Program (IEP) is an individually tailored education plan that represents the promise of special education and is the foundation of special education law and practice. An IEP must be developed annually for every student with a disability who receives special education and related services under the Individuals with Disabilities Education Act (IDEA). It must contain the goals and objectives to be achieved as well as the specialized interventions that are to be provided. The IEP is supposed to be based on a careful assessment of the individual student and should be the culmination of a planning process that is both multidisciplinary and involves families.

The recent significant changes that have been made to the IEP documents and processes are intended to promote greater access to general education curriculum for students with disabilities. New components of IDEA emphasize making the IEP a meaningful instructional and planning tool by focusing on students' participation in general education standards and curriculum. These requirements include the following:

- Statements of a child's present level of educational performance to specify how his or her disability affects involvement and progress in the general curriculum

- Measurable annual goals including short-term objectives or new benchmarks that must be designed to enable the child to be involved, and progress, in the general curriculum

- A statement of the special education and related services as well as the supplementary services that will be provided to the child

- Any program modifications or supports for school personnel necessary for the child to advance appropriately toward the annual goals, to progress in the general curriculum, and to be educated and participate with other children with disabilities and nondisabled children

- An explanation from IEP team members of the extent, if any, to which the child will *not* participate with nondisabled children in the regular class and activities

The importance of large-scale assessments as an accountability mechanism to support standards-based reform did not escape attention in the IDEA amendments of 1997. IEP's must include a statement of any individual modifications in the administration of state or district-wide student achievement assessments that are needed in order for the child to participate. If the IEP team determines that a child will not participate in a specific state or district-wide assessment, the team must document why that assessment is not appropriate for the child and how the child will be assessed using alternate methods.

The new components are intended to focus on how a student will access the general education curriculum, but they do not demote the importance of making individual decisions about students and their instructional needs. The challenge for special educators is how to make those individualized decisions within the context of a common general curriculum. This chapter will present a decision-making process for thinking about how a student will access the general education curriculum and it will address each of the key IEP components.

Thinking of Curricular Access on a Continuum

Two terms that are widely used in the development of the new IEPs are *accommodations* and *modifications* (or sometimes referred to as *adaptations*). It is important that teachers understand the differences between these two terms and how they apply to IEP decision making.

Before reviewing accommodations and modifications, access to the general education curriculum needs to be considered along the continuum we presented in Figure 1.1 in the first chapter. That is, IEP planning for each child begins with the assumption that the student will be taught the subject matter defined by the general education curriculum *regardless of the setting or environment where the student is being educated.* For some students, such as those receiving only speech and language services, no changes may be necessary to the content or the instruction that is provided within the general curriculum.

The next level of access on the continuum assumes that instructional accommodations will be made, but that the student will be expected to learn all of the curriculum content as other peers in the classroom. Curricular modifications begin to change the expectations regarding content as well as learner achievement and outcomes. Finally, a totally individualized set of content goals may be defined for a few students. To understand the continuum, teachers must clearly understand the nature of the curriculum as we discussed in Chapter 3, "The Learning-Teaching Connection," and be clear about the larger learnings associated with the content domain. Teachers must be able to differentiate curriculum content from instruction, have a firm understanding of a student's current level of performance, and know the difference between accommodations and modifications.

Accommodations

An accommodation typically is defined as a service or support that is provided to help a student fully access the subject matter and instruction as well as to validly demonstrate what he or she knows. An accommodation does not change the content of instruction nor the performance expectations. Accommodations should not interfere with or markedly change the standards specified for students. That means that a student is expected to learn to a defined level of mastery all of the information that typical students will learn.

A new and important addition to IEP planning is the need to develop accommodations in the areas related to a child's disability across *all* of the general education curriculum. That is, if a student has a reading disability, teachers must plan for how they will accommodate or support the student's reading in all subject matter content, including math, science, art, and so on, that requires reading, without altering the curricular goals or expected student learning outcomes.

Accommodations can be as simple as pencil grips, large-print books, or changing a student's setting to a more quiet place. More marked accommodations could include allowing a student more time to complete an assignment or test, allowing calculators or spell checkers, or allowing students to use simple word-processing software for written assignments. Accommodations also can include providing more practice of specific skills, more opportunities for applying skills or concepts, and direct instruction in using specific knowledge in different contexts. In fact, increasing a student's opportunity to learn by increasing the time allocated to instruction and providing specific instructional strategies may be among the most powerful accommodations teachers can make.

Deciding on accommodations requires that teachers have a sound knowledge of the key goals of a specific lesson or instructional unit such that they understand that the accommodation does not alter the big idea or major learning outcomes expected of the instruction. Again, it is vital for teachers to have or work with a colleague who has a deep understanding of the content domain. In general, accommodations fall into three categories: alternative acquisition modes, content enhancements, and alternative response modes.

Alternative Acquisition Modes

The purpose of alternative acquisition strategies is to augment, bypass, or compensate for a motor, sensory or information processing deficit (Lewis, 1993). Decisions to provide these kinds of accommodations most likely will involve a multidisciplinary team that includes therapists (occupational, physical, speech) or other specialists with expertise in adaptive technology. A complete discussion of the range of adaptive supports available for students who have motor, sensory, or cognitive deficits is beyond the scope of this book, but it is likely that most teachers are familiar with some alternative acquisition tools of one form or another. These accommodations can include sign language interpreters, Braille materials, voice-output computers, and tape-recorded books.

Content Enhancements

Students who have learning problems often need assistance managing the strategic aspects of learning, and *content enhancements* can help in this area. Content enhancements were described by Lenz, Bulgren, and Hudson (1990) as techniques that help students identify, organize, comprehend, and remember content information. Content enhancements can include a number of supports with which many teachers already are familiar, including these examples (Hudson, Lignugaris-Kraft, and Miller, 1993):

- **Advance organizers**: These are pre-instructional materials designed to enhance students' linkage of new information with prior knowledge stored in long-term memory. Advance organizers may be verbal, written, or be presented in a question format. Examples could include questions presented prior to a discussion or reading assignment, vocabulary words presented on the board or a handout, or verbal statements presented by the teacher designed to activate knowledge prior to instruction.

- **Visual displays**: These include diagrams, concrete models, videos, or digital material designed to portray the relationships among various pieces of information presented during instruction. Visual displays are intended to help students organize information in long-term memory as well as to activate prior knowledge during instruction. They function as an accommodation to the extent that they scaffold the creation of linkages among information in the learner's long-term memory. Examples could include diagrams, graphic organizers, concept maps, or video segments intended to anchor or situate the student's learning (Harley, 1996) in a meaningful context.

- **Study guides**: These consist of worksheets that are provided to the student prior to a reading or study assignment. They include a set of statements or questions intended to focus the student's attention and cognitive resources on the key information to be learned. Study guides can take the form of completed or partially completed outlines, questions focusing on the textual, literal, and inferential aspects of a study assignment, or various other tasks designed to prompt the active processing of the material to be studied.

- **Mnemonic devices**: These are techniques that assist in the storage and recall of declarative knowledge associated with content domains. Mnemonics may be verbal or pictorial and may be provided by the teacher or developed collaboratively by the teacher and the student. Most teachers are familiar with some of the common examples of mnemonics such as the use of key words, pictures, or symbols. ROY G BIV and Every Good Boy Deserves Fudge are classic mnemonic devices.

- **Peer-mediated instruction**: Here students are employed within the classroom as instructional agents. This form of content enhancement includes peer and cross-age tutoring, various forms of classwide tutoring, and cooperative learning. The primary purpose of peer-mediated instruction is to increase the number of opportunities for distributed practice with feedback. Usually, this approach entails fairly well-scripted or structured interactions designed and mediated by the teacher.

Alternative Response Modes

Expression serves a number of functions for students beyond simply answering questions and making their needs known. Formulating and expressing ideas is an integral part of the learning and assessment process. Therefore, it is important to find multiple ways for all students to express themselves in order to reduce barriers created by sensory or motor deficits or language differences. Of course, the way students most often communicate in classrooms is through speaking and writing, so whenever acceptable alternatives to those modes of expression can be employed, curriculum access is increased.

An example of a more specialized alternative response mode is the use of a scribe to transcribe a student's responses, such as when responding to test items. Often an instructional assistant (rather than another student) would serve in this role to ensure accurate, verbatim recording of the student's thoughts. Untimed response situations also can sometimes be used as an accommodation for students who need more time to complete work.

Modifications

When an instructional or curriculum modification is made, either the specific subject matter is altered or the performance expected of student is changed. A curriculum modification is made when a student either is taught something different from the rest of the class or is taught the same information but at a different level of complexity. For example, the rest of the class may be expected to tell the distinguishing characteristics of animal and plant cells, but a student for whom a modification has been made may simply be required to discriminate between animals and plants, given pictures and short descriptions.

A common modification offered to students is to reduce assignments by giving fewer problems or asking them to write one or two paragraphs instead of several pages. However, the effect of these types of modifications can be to "dumb down" the curriculum, to take away the difficult tasks and alter what students are expected to learn. In effect, these types of modifications can reduce a student's opportunity to learn the critical knowledge, skills, and concepts in certain subject matter. Therefore, modifications must be made within the context of the broad goals of the curriculum. We will discuss this further in the chapter when we address setting IEP goals.

Modifying *what* a student learns moves further along the continuum of curriculum access. A modification may begin by keeping the subject matter and essential curricular goals and objectives the same but changing the materials used in the lesson, such as providing lower level reading material. For example, some students in a language arts class may be reading literature at different reading levels, but all are working on identifying character development, plot, and "voice." More significant modifications occur as a teacher designs new material and tasks for individual children that mirror the general education curriculum in the broadest sense (for example, all of the students would be receiving math instruction, but the difficulty ranges from basic algebra to solving simple word problems). A similarly significant modification would be using a textbook or text in the same subject matter but that is below the grade level of the class. That is, some students may use a science textbook that is one or two grade levels below their assigned grade level. Using texts that are off-level not only reduces demand, but teaches very different concepts, vocabulary, and other key skills. The possible implications of this decision may be significant when curriculum variables discussed in Chapter 3 are considered. For example, it would be important to ensure that off-grade–level material does not interfere with the curriculum sequencing strategy and later result in the student having even greater gaps in prior knowledge than might otherwise be created from her or his learning deficit alone.

The decision to make an instructional modification is an important one and should not be made lightly or by one teacher acting alone. Modifications require a team decision. Curricular modifications have both long- and short-term implications. For example, some modifications may put the student at a great disadvantage on assessments and those assessments may have significant consequences for students as well as schools.

Teaching Less Content

Teaching less content implies that a student can get by without learning certain things. Frequently, teachers make this modification to help students keep up with classmates as they progress through segments of the curriculum. The assumption is that reducing content will bypass the student's learning problems. Be careful, though. Just because a student cannot keep pace with the curriculum or learn at the modal rate of the classroom does not always provide a good reason to reduce what a student will have a chance to learn or be held accountable for. Again, before reducing what a student learns, considerations for accommodations, such as more practice sessions or more intensive instruction, should be made.

Teaching Different Content

Teaching different content implies that the expected general curriculum outcomes are different for a particular student than for her or his classmates. The primary reason for making this modification is to provide instruction in content deemed important for the student that will not be taught in the general curriculum. For example, a student who needs more explicit instruction in "survival mathematics" may work in a different mathematics curriculum than others in the classroom. However, sometimes teaching specific skills or relevant content can be achieved by enhancing, not altering, what is taught in the general education classroom. For instance, students may need more explicit instructions in some daily tasks but may also receive instructions in the general curriculum goals as well.

Finally, at the most extreme end of the curriculum continuum are students whose curricular goals may be in areas outside of the general curricula (communication and social awareness) and whose instructional goals are individually tailored to reflect more functional life skills. For this small number of students who work in a more differentiated or expanded curriculum, access is defined more in terms of participation in curricular activities, but not necessarily in access to all of the same information or concepts.

Accommodations, Modifications, and Assessments

When teachers modify the curriculum for students with disabilities, they alter the link between instructions and assessment. Teachers need to be aware of what knowledge and skills are being assessed to determine whether, as they make modifications, they are maintaining the instructional focus on what students will need to do in the assessment.

Decisions to accommodate or modify curriculum have implications for how students will participate in state and district assessments. For example, if a student can fully access specific general education content without instructional accommodation, he/she should take whatever assessments are required in that subject matter without accommodations. Similarly, if a student receives an accommodation during instruction in a specific subject matter, the same accommodation should be provided during the assessment. Some standardized assessments currently being administered in school districts permit only certain accommodations. They restrict the use of all instructional accommodations that may be provided during instruction.

For those few students who may have very individualized learning goals, the use of an alternate assessment to the state or district assessment is the most appropriate and valid way to measure achievement.

Special Education and Related Services

As Figure 1.1 showed, for every student with an IEP, there is an expectation that special education and related services will be provided to meet his/her unique needs. The decisions to provide related services may not impact decisions regarding a student's access to the general curriculum or they may serve as important accommodations. For some students who receive speech therapy to correct articulation or fluency difficulties, curriculum access may not be an issue. Others may require specialized therapies that may help them with writing or other motor functions and accommodate instruction. Of course, some intensive related-service goals for students with the most significant disabilities become part of a very different curriculum. Assistive technology, transition services, and the specialized supports provided to students with visual or hearing impairments all are part of the mix of individual services and supports to be considered as part of IEP planning.

Special education interventions refer to the full array of instructional assessments, strategies, accommodations, and supports that are offered to help a student meet his/her IEP goals. Special education and related services may occur within or outside of the general education classroom and are not influenced by the degree to which a student is "accessing" the general education curriculum. In other words, students who may be pursuing all or most of the general education curricular goals may need as much or as intensive special education services as students with very different curricular goals.

The intent of the IEP is that each student will receive an individualized assessment of educational performance that will lead to individualized goals, objectives, and instructions, but these goals must be based on the general curriculum. Individualizing goals, objectives, and instructions within the context of providing access to the general education curriculum is among the more difficult tasks that IEP teams now face. The following decision model presents a process for developing IEP's. Key questions and considerations are presented to help the IEP team engage in individual planning for special education students.

Key IEP Components: Challenges for Team Decision Making

Figure 5.1 provides a flow chart for thinking about the IEP development process as it relates to access to the general education curriculum.

The process we outline does not address every aspect of what IEP planning should involve and should not be confused with an actual IEP document. All school districts have established forms and procedures for developing IEPs that reflect the new IDEA requirements.

Although it is not possible for us to provide examples of the many IEP documents that can be found in schools, we can address the major tasks required in creating an individual student's IEP to provide access to the curriculum. These are assessments; specifications of goals, objectives, and benchmarks; specifying supplementary aids and supports; decisions about participation in large-scale assessments; and the setting where instruction is to take place.

Instructional Assessment

The IEP process begins with an analysis of a student's present performance in the general education curriculum. As we consider assessment

Figure 5.1   The Decision-making process: Standards and the IEP

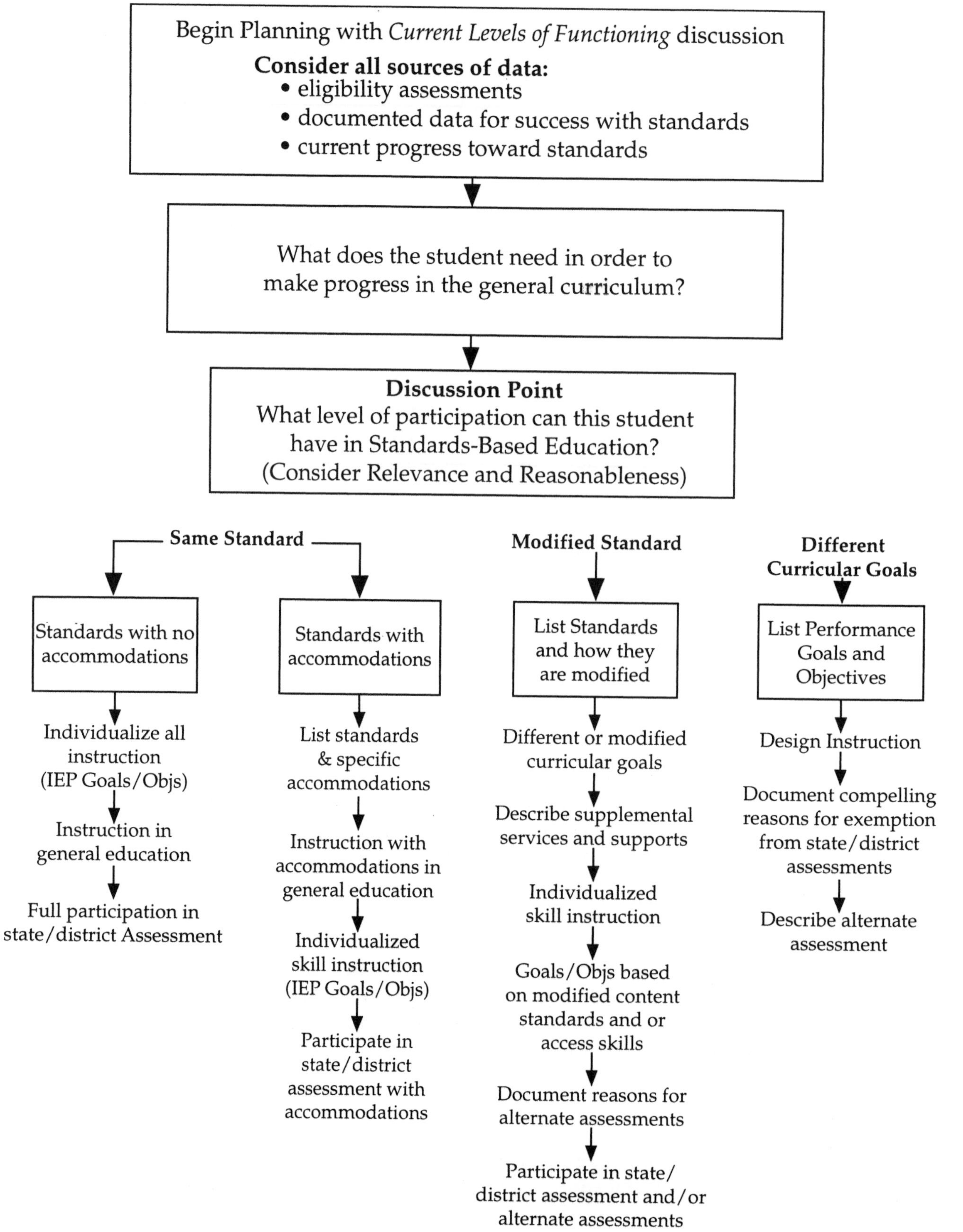

Begin Planning with *Current Levels of Functioning* discussion

Consider all sources of data:
- eligibility assessments
- documented data for success with standards
- current progress toward standards

What does the student need in order to
make progress in the general curriculum?

Discussion Point
What level of participation can this student
have in Standards-Based Education?
(Consider Relevance and Reasonableness)

Same Standard

Standards with no accommodations	Standards with accommodations

Individualize all instruction (IEP Goals/Objs)

Instruction in general education

Full participation in state/district Assessment

List standards & specific accommodations

Instruction with accommodations in general education

Individualized skill instruction (IEP Goals/Objs)

Participate in state/district assessment with accommodations

Modified Standard

List Standards and how they are modified

Different or modified curricular goals

Describe supplemental services and supports

Individualized skill instruction

Goals/Objs based on modified content standards and or access skills

Document reasons for alternate assessments

Participate in state/district assessment and/or alternate assessments

Different Curricular Goals

List Performance Goals and Objectives

Design Instruction

Document compelling reasons for exemption from state/district assessments

Describe alternate assessment

here, we are assuming that an evaluation to determine eligibility has already occurred and that the adverse educational impact of the student's disability has been identified. Assessment information now must be collected to inform educational planning for the student. This first step toward access requires a very different perspective when looking at student learning and student achievement. Teachers must define the student's current level of performance in all of the curricular areas that are deemed to be impacted by the disability. This analysis must examine more than simple skills and must include concepts as well as more complex thinking skills. In Chapter 4, "Evaluating the Outcomes of Access," we discussed the tools for evaluating how a student is performing and functioning in the curriculum. Remember the challenge is to not to fall into the trap of thinking that because a student has not mastered a basic skill, he or she is not ready to use knowledge in more complex operations.

Of course, knowledge of the curriculum is essential to this assessment. The decision framework for finding the general curriculum presented at the end of Chapter 3 will help here. Application of that analysis in the context of IEP development entails a three-phase process:

Phase 1: Identify the critical, enduring knowledge associated with the general curriculum that all students will learn.

Phase 2: Analyze the key knowledge and skills that a competent individual uses to perform tasks associated with that enduring knowledge. This step is generally analogous to the process of task analysis familiar to many special educators, except that it does not involve the kind of fine-grained molecular analysis that often results in irrelevant goals and objectives focused on small subcomponents of basic skills. Remember the whole is bigger than the sum of the parts when we are talking about the kind of generative thinking and problem-solving that is the goal of the general curriculum.

Phase 3: Analyze the individual child's use of key learning processes and strategies discussed in Chapter 3. This analysis may involve some of the assessment tools discussed in the last chapter as well as a more general analysis of the learning processes involved in acquisition and use of the information to be learned.

Some questions that can guide this analysis include the following:

- **What will "typical" students be expected to do (math, science, reading, PE, and so on) during the timeframe addressed by the IEP (this grading period, semester, year)?** Define the student performances expected.

Examples include being able to read specific text independently and answer questions, be able to accurately estimate size and measurement in a variety of daily situations, and write a minimum of four paragraphs that logically develop an idea while conforming to rules of grammar and punctuation.

* **How is the target student currently performing in these areas?** Look at classroom evidence regarding the key areas as well as input from parents, teachers, and other team members. The criterion-referenced assessment strategies we discussed in the last chapter will be useful here. The idea is to decide where the student falls on a continuum of competence in the particular domain of interest.

* **In what ways are the student's disabilities impacting the performance?** In addition to specific skill deficits such as in reading or math, educational assessments should consider such things as attention or focus, organizational skills, and other learning processes?

The outcome of this assessment is clear ideas regarding the road map for learning that must be developed for an individual student. The IEP team is now ready to set goals, objectives, and benchmarks.

Goals, Objectives, and Benchmarks

IEP goals and objectives should be the targets that individual students need to reach by the end of an instructional year. The goals should be clear enough to focus instruction and be evaluated yet broad and balanced enough in order to not limit what is expected or taught. Instructional objectives are more discrete stops on the way toward the eventual target, while benchmarks are broader, perhaps linked to grading periods or other natural breaks in an academic calendar. The parts of an instructional objective are described in Box 5.1. If you need more information about how to develop effective instructional objectives, you should consult Robert F. Mager's *Preparing Instructional Objectives: A Critical Tool in the Development of Effective Instruction* (1997).

Teachers should consider two key elements when setting performance targets in IEPs. First, while IEPs are reviewed annually, teachers should think about the longer time frames that are defined within the general education curriculum. For example, planning for individual students should include determining what topics students in general education are expected to learn during a particular time period (such as a unit, a grading period, or a semester), over one academic year, and over several years (such as grades K-3).

Thinking about the multi-grade benchmarks is important for several reasons. First, special education teachers must keep their eyes on what all

Box 5.1   Anatomy of an Instructional Objective

The terms "goal" and "objective" often are used interchangeably. Goals indicate the long-term outcomes expected to result from instruction, and objectives are the interim steps along the way. In classroom applications, goals usually have an annual focus and objectives generally reflect what is expected to occur in the next quarter. Content and performance standards in state and district curriculum frameworks can be thought of as goals that have a one- to three-year focus. Regardless of their time focus, all goals and objectives answer the following questions:

Who?	*Will do?*	*What?*	*How well?*	*Under what conditions?*

Who?	Specifies who will be expected to accomplish the goal.
Will do?	An action verb that can be observed when executed.
What?	Tells *specifically* what the student will do.
How well?	Specifies the minimum standard you establish for accomplishing the goal. If this standard is not met, the goal has not been accomplished.
Under what conditions?	Indicates the context in which the goal will be observed. This is an indication of the level of difficulty. For example, "in three minutes on a test" represents a very different set of conditions than "overnight for homework."

Here is an example of a quarterly objective you might develop for a student learning to incorporate peer feedback into a final essay draft:

Roger	will write	a final version of a creative essay	with no spelling or punctuation errors	after his writing partner has proofread his first draft.
Who?	*Will do?*	*What?*	*How well?*	*Under what conditions?*

Instructional objectives originally were championed by educators working in the behaviorist tradition. This has led some teachers to believe that instructional objectives are not appropriate for dimensions such as student attitudes or thinking skills that cannot be readily observed. Although it is true that not all important educational outcomes can be measured directly, objectives *can* be written for effective or covert cognitive operations. To do so, think about how you would know your instruction has been effective and how the desired change in thinking has occurred. For example, suppose you want your student to develop an appreciation for various genres of writing (essay, biography, science fiction, romance). Here is a quarterly objective you might write:

During the next two months . . .

Diane	will select	at least three different types	of reading	when given a choice during free time.
Who?	*Will do?*	*What?*	*How well?*	*Under what conditions?*

students are expected to know and demonstrate on the key state and local assessments. These assessments are typically administered around the fourth, eighth, and eleventh grades. However, these grade levels can differ across districts and across tests. What is important for teachers to consider is that large-scale assessments are intended to measure what a student has learned over a period of several years. Achievement and learning are cumulative. Teachers cannot afford to set goals that reflect very fragmented or discrete learner expectations over limited time periods, such as one year. These types of goals will not move the student forward toward the larger sets of knowledge, skills, and applications that will be expected on the assessment.

Defining Goals and Objectives: The Challenge

Let's now walk through the decision-making process shown in Figure 5.1. Past practices in special education and IEP development, as we discuss in previous chapters, have frequently focused on measuring the discrete skill deficits of a student with a disability and analyzing the skill to identify small teachable units. The specific skill is frequently the annual IEP goal and the small tasks or teachable units are then translated into IEP objectives. These practices, based on assumptions that learning is hierarchical and that learning more complex knowledge and skill depends on the mastery of all former skills, will not work for the type of learning we now expect of students. Nor will these approaches to defining goals and objectives match the type of instruction that is expected of teachers as part of the new content standards.

Step 1: Do We Need a Goal?

In our IEP process, annual goals, objectives, and benchmarks are defined only in areas where there is specialized instruction or where there is modification of a curricular goal or student performance expectation. That is, if a student is expected to demonstrate knowledge of the same skills and content with or without instructional accommodations, no goals are required. However, the supports and accommodations as well as individuals responsible for providing those supports must be clearly described in the IEP.

Individualized IEP goals should be specified for related services as well as in areas outside of the general curriculum where the student may be receiving specialized instruction. For example, specific speech, occupational or physical therapy goals may be specified. In addition, behavioral goals and supports, specific learning strategies that may be taught, or other skills that are outside of the general curriculum need to be addressed.

The important questions are as follows:

* What do we expect the student to be able to do at the end of this instructional year? The list of targets encompasses both general curriculum as well as specialized knowledge and skill areas.

* Do we expect the student to be able to demonstrate the same performances and outcomes in the subject matter as the typical student?

* Will the student need accommodations? If so, which ones? Which alternative methods will the student receive? Instruction may be provided in addition to that delivered to others or it may be used instead of the classroom instruction. For example, a student may receive reading instructions through a more explicit approach than other students in the class.

There may also be additional opportunities for reteaching using more representations and for practice. Of course, a number of other accommodations as defined earlier may also be provided.

• What specialized interventions will be required?

Remember IEP planning should *begin* with the assumption that every student has the same goals as those in the general education curriculum. This assumption requires that the special education teacher understand the short-term goals (such as the units of instruction for a particular grade level) as well as the long-term goals within the subject or discipline. We previously discussed that goals of the new curriculum stress high-order thinking including manipulating and using information in new ways, deep knowledge that includes complex understanding of content, and the ability to connect school knowledge to the world beyond. To answer the questions posed above, the IEP team will need a comprehensive assessment of student performance within the general curriculum.

The IEP must specify the accommodations that will be provided to support progress toward the general education curriculum goal. We will talk about how to design more universal instructional accommodations and processes later in this chapter. Finally, before moving to consider modifying a curricular goal, the team should consider if all possible accommodations, including increasing the opportunity to learn, have been made.

Step 2: Setting IEP Goals for Modifications or Different Curriculum

If the IEP team determines that curricular goals must be modified, the first step is to consider the subject matter or content requiring modifications. Goals need only be specified in those areas. Both general and special educators as well as parents must consult and collaborate on the decisions to modify. Educators must determine which of the overall general education curricular goals the individual student will be expected to learn. However, it is extremely important that all members of the team consider how the changes in content reduce the student's opportunity to learn certain knowledge and how that may impact assessment performances.

Setting these types of IEP goals requires what we earlier referred to as a sort of "educational triage," wherein the teachers must decide on the key or critical knowledge within a specific set of content that the student must learn. The following section discusses some key questions when making these decisions.

• **Will we teach the same content but lower the performance expectation?**
Here the decision is to expose the student to all of the same knowledge

and instruction that is provided to the typical student, but to reduce the expectations of what the student will have to demonstrate. This decision is very much related to teaching less content but assumes that the student should receive instruction in all of what is taught, but he or she will only be expected to learn less.

This is a tricky modification because it assumes that instructional time and other resources will be devoted to fitting the student into all of the classroom instruction, but that they won't have to do as much. However, in reducing assignments or assessment expectations, teachers are at risk of making ad hoc decisions that in fact result in students learning less. For example, requiring a student to only answer half of a set of questions or complete only a subset of math problems may mean that some important knowledge of applications is neither stressed nor assessed.

- **Will we teach less content?** The decision is to reduce the amount of content that a student will be explicitly taught is different from teaching the same content but changing the performance expectations. There are a variety of ways to make this modification: the student learns fewer objectives or curricular benchmarks, the student completes shorter units or parts of a unit, the student reads fewer pages, or paragraphs, or the student participates in shorter lessons or parts of lessons.

The key considerations for reducing content determine the most enduring knowledge within the broad curriculum goals specified for a given grade level or across multiple grade levels. The role of standards in this process cannot be underestimated. The purpose of content standards is to define that critical set of knowledge. It is important to understand that teachers will include instructional objectives and activities in their units of instruction and lesson plans beyond the core. If the IEP team must determine what to teach, it should first be the essential core of knowledge that educators believe all students should learn, not just those that are the easiest to teach. In addition to standards, the examples we provided in Chapter 3 are helpful in making decisions about what to teach.

Box 5.2 shows an example of how goals and standards should be related.

The modified goals in the example in Box 5.2 are only two of perhaps as many as 10 or 12 that define the general education curriculum goals of one fourth-grade math standard related to spatial sense, measurement, and geometry. It is obvious from this example that the process of goal setting can become enormously complex and time-consuming if teachers approach the IEP development as a parallel of the general education standards and curriculum goals.

Instead, special education teachers need to be familiar with the underlying intent of the standard and the goals, in particular the types of

Box 5.2   Relationship of Goals to Standards

Standard: The learner will demonstrate an understanding and be able to apply the properties and relationships in geometry and standard units of measurement.

General Education Curricular Goal: Use manipulatives, pictorial representations, and the appropriate vocabulary to identify properties of polyhedra in the environment.

Modified Goal: Use a variety of manipulatives, pictures, and real-life objects to demonstrate the properties and shapes of familiar objects in the students' home and school environments.

General Education Curricular Goal: Estimate and measure length, capacity, and mass using these units: inches, yards, miles, centimeters, meters, kilometers, milliliters, cups, pints, kilograms, and tons.

Modified Goal: Estimate and measure length, area, capacity of familiar objects, and places in the students' home and school environments using inches, cups, and pints.

broad student skills and competencies expected as an outcome of instruction. From these expectations, they must then develop annual goals that align with the standard and reflect the desired broad student performance intended in the standard.

- **Will the student need accommodations?** If so, which ones? Think about the critical effect an accommodation will have. Is there an accommodation that can augment existing skills and abilities? Can an accommodation compensate for or bypass the student's disability without altering the learning task itself?

- **What specialized interventions will be required?** Remember IEP goals must consider additional skills and knowledge areas beyond the general curriculum that must be addressed through special education. These goals will also need to be specified.

- **Will we set alternative goals?** As we have previously noted, every student could have some IEP goals that reflect specific skills or knowledge that is required to address the impacts of the disability. However, with respect to alternative curriculum goals, we refer to those few students who are working toward an individualized set of instructional goals or objectives, either within the same subject matter areas as their peers or in different areas.

For example, a student in a middle school science class might focus on specific content reading strategies, rather than learning certain science facts and concepts. A student may also complete different instructional units either occasionally or on a regular basis. For example, during the time a class is working on a unit on electricity and magnetism, the student might complete a unit on personal safety with electricity. The student might use a different set of instructional materials than is used by the rest of the class. For example, a student with reading problems might use so-called "high-interest, low-demand" textbooks.

Whatever the intent, the IEP goals should be parsimonious and clear. That is, they should communicate to parents, all of the student's teachers, and to the student him- or herself what they will be expected to learn in specific subject matter areas during specific timeframes. IEP goals should also be attainable within the constraints of the instructional time and the instructional environments available to the student. Broad and extensive goal statements are not productive targets. Teachers should be less concerned about how elegantly the goals are stated and focus more on how accurate an instructional target they are. The elements of immediacy and specificity discussed in Chapter 2, "Understanding What Curriculum Is," should be considered here.

The IEP goals should also translate easily into assessments that clearly indicate to teachers how students are progressing and whether instructional changes are necessary. Finally, IEP goals should also be rigorous and relevant. They should not be mired in low-level skills. However, at the same time, they should reflect both the important learning processes discussed in earlier chapters as well as the critical basic literacy and functional skills that may be essential to a student's future.

Objectives and Benchmarks

Much has been written about developing instructional objectives. In the 1997 changes to IDEA, a new term, *benchmarks*, was added to the IEP components. Some confusion has existed over the difference between an objective and a benchmark. In fact, some of the discussions surrounding how to improve the IEP have focused on eliminating the need for objectives, as they were creating the narrow and often limited perspective of special educators on what to teach students with disabilities. The argument is that if we eliminate IEP objectives, we might create more rigorous and more challenging instruction in the important subject matter of the general education curriculum.

Objectives can provide important information to parents and students, as well as teachers, about the specifics of what will be taught. Objectives create the map to the larger performance targets or instructional goals. However, recall that in Chapter 2 we discussed the balance that must be struck between establishing highly observable and measurable objectives and larger, more general statements of curriculum outcomes. Using benchmarks is one way to strike this balance.

Benchmarks are the stops along the way to the goal. They are the exemplars of performance expected at key points during the school year. For general educators, these frequently translate into instructional units or blocks of instruction delivered during a grading period or semester. In Box 5.1, the goals would also have critical benchmarks and indicators. For example, the student might be expected to use the linear measures to compute the length, width, and distance of a variety of real objects by the end of the first grading period. These would be followed by benchmarks addressing other measurement skills for the next period and so forth. If a teacher wanted more specificity, objectives could be written in conjunction with the benchmarks.

Again, using the analogy of a road map, if you are starting in New York and driving to Los Angeles, you would need to project where you will be each night. The route you take or the speed you choose may be determined when you begin, much as you set objectives. However, each day you monitor your progress and adjust your objectives. So too must the IEP provide the map from which teachers, parents, and students design their journey of learning. The key idea to remember in setting the goals is that they should be clear performance targets that can be broken into manageable pieces and that clearly define expected student performances relative to specific content standards. Further, the annual goals should be clearly aligned with and link to multi-year performance targets that are defined by local and state assessments.

Specifying the Link Between Goals and Assessments

The link between setting IEP goals and state and district assessments is critical. First, considerations about accommodations should directly influence the decisions about assessment accommodations. Decisions made about goals are decisions that impact how prepared a student will be when the time comes for him or her to be assessed. If the assessments are used to make high-stakes decisions about schools and/or students, then goal setting cannot ignore the implications for assessments. Modified IEP goals may not address important subject matter that will be assessed. This may mean that a student will not receive a diploma or other consequences may result.

In our decision model in Figure 5.1, the specification of goals leads directly to decisions regarding participation in state or local assessments. It is the responsibility of the IEP team to ensure that the student will have a sufficient opportunity to learn what will be evaluated. However, if a decision is made to not provide instruction in the areas or at the expected performance levels of assessments, this decision must be informed by the knowledge of assessments and the consequences associated with those assessments.

Box 5.1 provides an anatomy of instructional objectives in a format that no doubt is familiar to many teachers. However, a word of caution is in order here. The traditional way of writing IEP objectives, with some reference to the percentage of mastery, will not be useful for creating goals pertaining to complex thinking and problem-solving. For example, what would it mean to say that a student is able to "write a descriptive paragraph with 85 percent accuracy?" Instead, IEP teams must think about objectives as a way of locating a student on some continuum of performance. Over time, the student would be expected to move along the continuum in the direction of expertise. This approach requires two changes the way IEP teams think about the link between goals and assessments.

First, the assessment process used for developing IEP goals must generate multiple forms of evidence of the student's level of performance. This body of evidence should consist primarily (if not entirely) of classroom-based and curriculum-based measures, rather than formal tests. Minimally, before writing a goal, a team will want to collect multiple samples of the student's work or performance in a variety of relevant and meaningful contexts. For example, before developing a written expression goal, various samples of writing on worksheets, journals, and letters might be collected pertaining to social studies, math, and language arts. The team also would want to obtain information pertaining to the student's use of the targeted knowledge or skill from the student's parents (observations and expectations regarding writing) and current and past teachers.

Second, the continuum of competence against which the student's performance will be judged should be included in the IEP. When a goal refers to a scoring rubric that is not part of a published assessment system (such as a state performance assessment program), that rubric should be attached directly to the IEP. When a scoring rubric associated with established state or district assessments is used, this rubric can simply be referenced. For example, an IEP goal in mathematics for a middle school student might look like this:

Expected Outcome:

Willa will use variables in simple equations, inequalities, and formulas to solve two-step math problems.

Present Level of Performance:

On five separate occasions, when presented with two-step math problems requiring the use of variables, either developed by her teacher or sampled from the State Assessment Resource Kit, Willa's performance was scored by three different teachers at either a "0" or "1" on the state five-point scoring rubric for mathematics problem-solving.

Annual Goal:

By May 12, 2001, Willa's performance in solving two-step math problems requiring the use of variables will earn scores of "3" or "4" from at least three separate teachers using the state five-point scoring rubric for mathematics problem-solving.

From Goals to Instruction

The theory behind setting standards and designing instructional goals is that they will drive changes in classroom instruction. As we see in the next chapter, this is neither easy nor automatic. However, changing how we teach students is an important aspect of guaranteeing access to the general education curriculum. We already have discussed aspects of designing instruction that matches the demands of new curricular standards. We have also addressed the important distinctions of accommodations and modifications. We noted how modifications can be made to goals based on a comprehensive assessment of a student's current status in the general education curriculum.

Before teachers begin to modify or change the performance expectations for students with disabilities, however, they must ensure that the overall conditions of instruction that exist in a classroom will enable students to achieve the standards. Therefore, we need to examine current classroom practices and materials to determine the degree of accommodation needed for student differences. Accommodations and modifications should be used only when the instruction in the general classrooms is unlikely to meet the needs of a particular student. To the maximum extent possible, the instructional environment in the classroom should eliminate the need for accommodations and modifications. One way to accomplish this goal is through the application of the principles of universal design.

Universal Design

Universal design refers to a "designed-in" flexibility to accommodate the instructional needs of many diverse learners in a single classroom (Orkwis and McLane, 1998). The underlying premise of universal design is that products and environments should be usable by the largest number of people possible without the need for additional modifications beyond those incorporated in the original design. When additional adaptations are needed, they should be easily and unobtrusively accommodated by the original design. Universal design implies that assistive supports are built-in, rather than added on as an afterthought. Architectural applications of universal design such as curb cuts, automatic doors, and integrated ramps have become common in new constructions in both the public and private sectors. These features now routinely are planned as integral elements during the design and blueprint phase of construction. A non-example of universal design would be the addition of a long, zigzagging plywood ramp to the side door of a recently constructed building after the original designers failed to consider the likelihood that someone with limited mobility would want to use the building.

Universal design requires that teachers consider the critical effects of their instructional decisions. As the principles of universal design become integral to the overall design process, decisions that have the effect of limiting access or usability for some individuals are replaced by designs that increase flexibility and accessibility. For example, as more architects embrace the principles of universal design, graceful, well-integrated ramps have become commonplace in new construction, and there is less need for those cobbled-together plywood appendages.

One of the key benefits of universal design is that the built-in features that accommodate individuals with disabilities make it easier for everyone else to use the product or environment. For example, OXO International manufactures a line of award-winning kitchen utensils that feature the Good Grips™, an ergonomically designed handle. These tools were engineered to be easily used by individuals who have limited mobility or strength in their hands, but they are popular because *most people* find them more comfortable than those with conventional handles. Indeed, most people who buy Good Grips™ products probably don't think of these traditional utensils as "accessible."

Applications of universal design in educational contexts generally have focused on designing physical and sensory means of access, primarily in electronic media and in computer hardware and software. For example, most personal computers routinely include controls that enable the user to customize the speed of mouse and key commands, use alternative input keys, or turn auditory signals on and off. These capabilities are built in to the operating system, not added on later as an adaptation, and they are readily available for anyone who may want to use these features. Similarly, closed captioning decoders now are standard on most television sets and this feature is used by many more people than just those who are hard of hearing or deaf (Vanderheiden, 1996). It has become common to find televisions in noisy public areas such as restaurants and airport gates with closed captioning switched on.

One of the ways universal design accomplishes flexibility is through redundancy, that is, parallel systems that serve the same purpose. Access is increased when users can choose from among a range of options, those that best meet their needs or preference. Stairs and ramps both serve the same purpose. Closed captioning accomplishes the same purpose as the audio track on a television program. The choice offered by these redundant or parallel systems creates accessibility.

The principles of universal design can readily be applied to the design of instruction that accommodates individuals with cognitive disabilities. Such "universal design for learning" employs flexible curricular materials and activities that permit a wide range of learners to accomplish challenging learning outcomes (Orkwis and McLane, 1998). The Center for Applied Special Technology (Rose, 1998) has summarized three essential principles of universal design for learning. Notice how the idea of flexibility through redundancy is central to these principles:

1. **Provide multiple means of representation.** This means that information should be available in more than one format. For example, captions should be provided for audio material and relevant descriptors should be provided for graphics and video. Whenever possible, text should be provided in digital format along with the printed version to permit transformations of variables such as size, color, shape, and spacing.

2. **Provide multiple means of expression.** This means that students should have comparable alternatives for communicating and demonstrating what they have learned as well as for interacting with the instructional system. For example, instead of writing a response with pencil and paper, a student could perform the same activity on a computer, through speaking, or graphically through the use of drawings, illustrations, or photography.

3. **Provide multiple means of engagement.** This means that all students are appropriately challenged by the content and format of the curriculum. For example, scaffolding is provided for those students who need it, and the amount of repetition built into instructions is matched to the learning rate of each student. At the same time, the instruction includes opportunities for all students to be challenged sufficiently for learning to occur.

A universal design for learning implies that information will be presented in multiple ways, students will be able to express themselves in multiple ways, and students will be given multiple pathways for engaging in the curriculum. The purpose of building in this flexibility is to eliminate the effects of any learning barriers that are created when students have sensory, motor, cognitive, or language differences. The sections that follow provide specific strategies for incorporating the principles of universal design into day-to-day planning and teaching.

Multiple Means of Representation

No single best way exists for presenting information in order to provide equal access for all learners. Indeed, a method that facilitates access for one individual may actually limit access for another (Orkwis and McLane, 1998). For example, a math lesson taught in Spanish would improve access for those students who speak Spanish as their first language but limit access for non-Spanish speakers. However, designs that build in flexibility through redundant or parallel systems will be less likely to present barriers than those designs that rely on a single representation strategy.

Teaching Presentations

Redundancy in teaching presentations means *more than once in different ways*. The grid in Figure 5.2 illustrates various ways teachers can employ more than one format for presenting information. Of course, it won't always be possible to present all information in redundant formats,

Figure 5.2   Redundancy in teaching presentations

Redundant Representation Formats			
Say it	**Show it**	**Model it**	**Different media**
Lecture	Pictures/graphics	Demonstrate	Video tape/disc
Discussion	Transparency	Think aloud	Audio tape/disc
Questioning	White board	Act out	Computer
Read aloud	Video	Build/construct	Television
Verbal descriptions	Captions	Manipulatives	Manipulatives

but the more cells on the grid you can employ simultaneously to present information, the more access will be built into your presentation. For example, if your primary mode for presenting new information is through lecture and discussions, you could employ a video with captioning that presents the same information or construct a model to show key relationships.

Instructional Materials

As a general principle, designs that employ digital text are more desirable than those that rely only on printed text (Orkwis and McLane, 1998). Digital text is highly flexible because its shape, size, color, and contrast can be transformed easily to accommodate students whose perceptual or cognitive deficits interfere with their ability to obtain information from printed materials. Although relatively few of the materials routinely used in classrooms are available in digital form, publishers and material developers have recognized that a huge demand exists for instructional material in a digital format. More instructional materials will soon be available in electronic form, either as stand-alone products or in networked environments. In the meantime, some options are available, albeit of the "plywood appendage" variety. Some instructional materials can be scanned electronically and then presented to students in a digital format, although this may not be an acceptable solution when the materials contain many graphics or unusual characters that cannot be interpreted by optical character recognition software.

When instructional materials include information presented in an audio format (for example, a videotape), redundancy should be built in through captioning or transcripts to enable students who have hearing impairments to gain access to the information. Similarly, when information is presented graphically or pictorially, verbal descriptions should be provided for those students who are blind, have low vision, or who would benefit from more explicit presentations of the material. The number and variety of video materials available with descriptive video is increasing rapidly and should be selected whenever possible.

Multiple Means of Expression

The principles of universal design imply that teachers should allow students to select the form of expression that best meets their needs from an menu of options. Here are some examples of alternative modes of expression students could use to express themselves throughout the learning process.

Presentation and Graphics Software

A number of computer software applications enable the user to organize information into slides that can later be presented electronically, printed, or transformed into overhead transparencies. Using this software, a learner who has difficulty either writing or speaking can express quite complex ideas and relationships with relatively little writing and no speaking. Using the clip-art, graphics, and formatting tools, a user could even create polished-looking finished products that contain no writing but readily express ideas and demonstrate learning. Computer applications for drawing sketches and illustrations also have become commonplace and often are integrated into word-processing software found on most computers. Students who are physically limited in their writing abilities can use these applications in lieu of other means of expression.

Oral Presentation

Oral presentations are commonly used in some classrooms, but teachers may not view them as alternatives to traditional means of expression. Students who may not be able to write can present information to the entire class, in small groups, or by speaking one on one. Oral presentations can be made more effective when the teacher structures the task for students who may need assistance organizing ideas. Also, using other materials in conjunction with an oral presentation can simplify the process. For example, rather than writing a paragraph, a student could create a poster and then describe it. Of course, the computer software described previously also could be helpful here.

Models and Manipulatives

Often it is possible to structure tasks and activities so that students can construct models or use simple manipulatives to express ideas or communicate learning. Familiar examples of this strategy include using Styrofoam balls and toothpicks to build a model of a molecule or creating a model of the solar system using strings and balls. However, students can express themselves in many other ways using simple manipulatives. Not only does this strategy enable students who have limited means of expression to communicate, but it can also support the transfer of knowledge and the development of abstract or analogical reasoning, particularly when simple, readily available manipulatives are used.

Flexible Means of Engagement

As we have emphasized throughout this book, access to the general curriculum implies that all children should have the opportunity to attain challenging content and performance standards. It is likely that most teachers would agree with the philosophy of this premise that the "all" should include students who have sensory or motor deficits that interfere with access to the curriculum. Most teachers also would support this assertion that the "all" should includes students from minority language or cultural groups as well. What is troublesome for many teachers, though, is the idea of accommodating students who have cognitive barriers to participation in the curriculum. Accommodating these students often is interpreted as "watering down" the curriculum and is viewed as somehow being unfair to the other students in the class who manage to achieve "on their own."

However, when students have multiple ways to be engaged in the curriculum, it is possible for students of differing abilities and backgrounds to be comparably challenged by the same content. One way to accomplish this goal is through attention to the format of the information you are teaching (facts, concepts, principles, or procedures). Knowing what kind of information you are teaching can help you decide (a) how to teach it and (b) what students should do with it.

Recall that in the last chapter, we talked about the various cognitive processes students use to learn and remember different kinds of information and the different kinds of intellectual activities that can be performed with various kinds of information. Students of differing abilities can be comparably challenged by the same content by being asked to perform different cognitive operations. For example, in a middle school science class, some students may be asked to *illustrate* the concept erosion by selecting from among several examples the one that best shows the concept. At the same time, others in the class might be asked to *evaluate* by telling which of two events is a better example of erosion and why.

Similarly, the instruction might provide different points of access for the same information. For example, a geography lesson about state government might include the following goals for different members of the class:

- Name our state capital (reiterate a fact)

- Give an example of a state capital (illustrate a concept)

- Tell the difference between a county and a state (evaluate a concept)

- Tell why states have capitals (apply a principle)

Chapter Summary

Special education policy is shifting to ensure that all students with disabilities have an opportunity to fully participate in the standards-based reforms now being implemented in U.S. schools. Key to the participation will be shifting the IEP process from one that considers the educational goals of a student with a disability in isolation to one that references individual plans within the broader demand of the general education curriculum. This chapter has provided a decision-making process and key considerations for IEP development in order to assist teachers in understanding what it means to create access to the general education curriculum.

It is important to remember that IEP development has always been a team process. Now, more than ever, the team is important to making good decisions about goals, accommodations, and modifications. Clearly, there will be a greater need for collaboration and communication among special and general educators in IEP development, regardless of where a student is educated. Knowledge of the larger goals of content standards and general education curricula is essential to IEP development. Furthermore, all teachers will need to become more adept at analyzing complex content in order to become more efficient at designing instruction that is universally accessible to *all* students. Parents and students themselves must be part of an informed decision-making process as well. Particularly, as access to general education curriculum affects the participation and performance on high-stakes assessments, it is important that these IEP team members know the implications of any modifications of standards or curricular goals.

6

CREATING THE
CONDITIONS FOR ACCESS

Throughout this book, we have been talking about the foundations for ensuring that all students have access to the general curriculum. Ensuring access requires a firm knowledge of subject matter and curriculum. Teachers must also have a firm understanding of the basic learning processes and how they influence the design of instruction. Ensuring access also requires skilled use of a variety of assessment tools to monitor students' progress toward accomplishing general education curriculum goals. Access is not just about placement in general education classrooms, nor can access be achieved through special education alone. Ensuring that all students have access to the general curriculum must involve communication and collaboration between special and general education teachers and administrators.

Recall that Figure 1.1 in the first chapter showed how access occurs on a continuum that involves more accommodations and modifications in the curriculum. Access means different things for different students. There is no single best definition of access, no single set of "things to do" to ensure access, or even one set of criteria for deciding how to provide access. Our own research involving high-reform schools indicates that the roles of general and special education teachers, administrators, and related service providers change as students move across the continuum of access. Therefore, the critical elements for ensuring that all students have meaningful access to the general curriculum are the conditions within a school that support the necessary access. Such conditions must possess the following characteristics:

- There must be an expectation that all students will benefit from having access to the general curriculum. All members of the school community must believe that the outcomes associated with the general curriculum are relevant and necessary for all students and that ensuring that each student has access to those outcomes is a worthwhile venture.

- Belief in the benefits of the general curriculum for all students must be grounded on the knowledge of the content standards and the expectations about what students must learn. Teachers and administrators must have a clear idea of what students will be expected to know and be able to do as a result of having had access to the curriculum.

- The school environment must promote flexibility and adaptability. The critical resources, such as teachers and time, must be able to change in response to student needs. Teachers must have time to learn from one another and the freedom to move around schedules to make optimal use of the available time and all of the expertise available in the school. In a flexible, adaptable school environment, many opportunities exist for doing business effectively to create a continuum of access. Remember, however, that there is always a finite amount of time and human resources. Therefore, time needs to be used wisely and efficiently, giving students the opportunity to learn the most important content.

In this chapter, we will illustrate how these conditions can support access by presenting four case studies of school districts engaged in major standards-based reform efforts. These real cases were developed as part of a large multiple-year study of four school districts that were implementing major educational reform initiatives. The research involved classroom observations and interviews with administrators, teachers, related service providers, and parents (McLaughlin, Henderson, and Rhim, 1997; McLaughlin, in press). We provide these descriptions to help you see how teachers interpret the meaning of "access" to standards and curriculum. We also discuss key findings about the conditions that support access to the curriculum derived from our interviews and observations in these reform schools.

Doyle County

Doyle County is a rapidly growing suburban county school system with over 24,000 students. About 92 percent of the student population is white, four percent are Hispanic, and three percent are Asian. The percentage of students receiving special education is eight percent and fewer than one percent are Title I-eligible. Two percent receive free and reduced price meals.

The county has been implementing a comprehensive set of interrelated reforms since the early 1990s. The system has developed a set of standards across all subject areas, and teachers have worked to develop a comprehensive set of assessments that include both norm-referenced and more performance-based artifacts. The standards and assessments are used for school accountability as well as to guide professional development and a pay-for-performance plan in the district. The county also has been very supportive of school choice and has several charter schools in the district.

State-level reforms include a set of standards and assessments that are administered at specific grade levels. The state reforms strike a balance between setting a core set of performance expectations for schools and supporting a great deal of local district autonomy and development. However, school performances on state and local assessments are publicly reported by each school and a concern exists over low performances. Everyone has become more aware of their school's test scores and the areas that need improvement.

Curriculum and Standards

Many teachers in Doyle County have been very involved in standards-writing and in translating standards into assessments. Instruction is guided by the standards, and teachers have many opportunities to discuss how to design lessons that are aligned with the standards. Teachers also feel comfortable with classroom assessments that measure the progress of students toward meeting the standards because they have been integrally involved in each school with developing various assessment practices that they can use. This work in assessments has been time-consuming but has helped teachers learn what a standard means in terms of a student's performance. "If he meets this standard, what kinds of things do we expect him to do?" The real push has been to focus on multiple tasks and assessments to create a body of evidence pertaining to each student.

The English and language arts standards are grounded in a whole language approach. Teachers at both elementary and middle schools are concerned about the number of poor readers, and principals note that reading is the area needing the most improvement on their assessments.

As a result, special education teachers provide phonics instruction to almost all students with mild to moderate disabilities as well as provide assistance to other slow readers. The middle schools recently added reading teachers who will provide phonemic instruction to poor readers.

Instructional Materials

Classrooms have a variety of materials, including a number of textbooks, reference materials, and trade books. Each classroom has at least two student computer work stations. The elementary classrooms have many manipulatives, games, and other instructional material. Student work, including many projects, is evident throughout the schools.

Teachers report that they feel very supported in their classrooms. They have the materials they need. They also feel that they have a strong professional development that is integrated with the standard and assessment development.

Students with Disabilities

The district has always had clear expectations that students with disabilities will be included in general education classrooms and assessments. Special and general education teachers collaborate in developing assessments and in designing lessons that provide students with access to the general education standards and curriculum. Special education teachers have been represented on all of the standards development teams.

Teachers use a variety of accommodations and modifications for students with varying disabilities. However, special education teachers usually design these and are often quick to modify or lower task demands for students. For example, students with disabilities almost always use different textbooks and often different materials (handouts and other teacher-made materials). Frequently, the worksheets and handouts are were modified on the spot for a particular student with a disability. Usually, this means crossing out certain questions or requiring fewer problems.

General and special education teachers feel that they have a good grasp of the needs and general performance levels of students with disabilities, based on their experience with the student in class and on the performance assessments they use. They rely less on the formal state or system assessments.

General and special education teachers actively collaborate in planning instructions. However, in most cases the general classroom teacher develops the specific lesson and activities. Special educators work with the teacher or, at the middle school, with the grade-level team to identify modifications and instructional strategies for individual students with disabilities. However, these modifications are not usually considered beyond a unit or a semester of instruction. They are not usually part of a larger plan that looks at curriculum goals across multiple years.

Classroom instruction frequently includes small groups, and students with IEPs, Sec. 504 accommodation plans, and other "at-risk" students tend to be grouped together. Their instruction is almost always provided or mediated by adults; there are few instances of peer "helpers." Adults usually include special education teachers, para-educators, and parent volunteers. These individuals are used flexibly, moving in and out of a classroom as needed. The classroom teacher also spends a large portion of his or her time "floating," keeping the low performing students on task, re-teaching, and/or giving corrective feedback. Among all teachers, there is a sense of urgency and almost a struggle to help each student keep pace with the curriculum.

A great deal of mutual respect exists among all teachers along with a sense of a professional community. There is also a sense of shared responsibility for students on IEPs with mild learning and behavior problems. For those students with more severe learning problems, including those with mental retardation, general educators are clearly in a supportive role and special educators design the curriculum, learner goals, and instruction. For many of these students, the focus is on participation in an inclusive classroom.

Hanley County

The Hanley County school district is a rural county school system that serves 7,500 students in 13 schools. About 90 percent of the students are white and nine percent are African-American. About 40 percent of the students receive free and reduced price meals and 12 percent receive special education.

This district is in a state with a rigorous standards-based educational reform package. State content and performance standards as well as a comprehensive set of assessments are driving school-level changes. School accountability is grounded in the assessment results and involve both sanctions and rewards for schools. Hanley County is considered to be in the top 20 percent of all districts in the state based on student performance on the state assessments.

State standards and assessments dominate the discussions among teachers and administrators. Teachers, both general and special education, support the notion of a common set of content standards. They believe that they unify the school and set high expectations for every student. However, teachers do not like the state assessments. The results of these assessments are used to hold schools accountable and determine both sanctions and monetary rewards. Improving assessment results monopolizes the attention of the schools. The stakes are perceived by the teachers to be very high. Almost all special education students are expected to fully participate in the assessments and their scores are included in the schools' accountability indices.

Many teachers resent the attention given to the assessments and to the pressure they feel they are under to improve results. Some say that the assessments are not valid, too subjective, not realistic, and demeaning to teachers. Special educators are concerned that the assessments don't allow their students to show what they really know.

Curriculum and Standards

The curriculum for the district is aligned with the state standards. The state has provided guidelines and extensive professional development to help schools and teachers translate the state standards into curriculum, actual units, and lesson plans. Teachers at the grade levels where assessments are administered are perhaps the most familiar with what knowledge and skills students are expected to have.

The emphasis on improving student performance is evident in the whole school approach to improvement. School planning is grounded in test results that determine most of a school's improvement goals. All resources are targeted at the same set of goals, and there is a common focus for professional development based on the school goals.

Teachers at the upper elementary and middle-level grades express concerns about the lack of fundamental skills, specifically reading and math computation, among many students. Teachers believe that these deficits are holding students back and contribute to the low test scores. They strongly believe that students must master these fundamental skills before they can engage in the types of higher-level problem-solving required by the state assessments. However, the information that is considered to be the enduring, fundamental knowledge associated with the curriculum varies among teachers. Most believe that these are basic math or reading literacy, but other teachers refer to learning processes or strategies such as memory.

Some upper-level teachers believe that teachers at the primary levels are not concerned enough about what students will be expected to do on the assessments and spend too much time on developmentally appropriate instructions and not skill acquisition.

Instructional Materials

Teachers have many materials, including manipulatives and computers. Junior high school classes are more traditional and use fewer computers, but multiple text, reference, and trade books are used. Almost every general education teacher relies on a textbook to check skill sequences and specific concepts (such as grammar and math concepts).

Classroom Instruction

A major emphasis exists across schools on improving instruction, and schools are adopting a particular model for differentiated instruction. As one teacher said, "There is a big push on 'how,' not 'what,' to teach."

Elementary instruction is a combination of whole groups and small groups, including peer tutors and cooperative learning groups. Teachers at the junior high school levels use more teacher-directed approaches, mostly lecture. The general lesson consists of whole group instruction, checking learning through questions and answers, and individual or small group assignments while the teachers "float" and check work or redirect.

Teachers evaluate student learning through traditional but informal means, such as grading assignments and questioning students. Teachers believe that they have a good grasp of what students need and what they should teach. However, some teachers spoke of being surprised by student performance on the state assessments because they varied from their experience.

Students with Disabilities

The state reforms have always explicitly included students with IEPs and 504 accommodation plans. In addition, the county has been part of a statewide systems change project focused on inclusion for a number of years. The inclusion of students with disabilities is supported by all teachers and is considered a given, yet most of the responsibility for teaching these students rests with special education teachers and/or para-educators.

General and special education teachers have frequent, often daily, opportunities for planning and collaboration. General education teachers make all or most of the decisions about daily lessons and activities, and special education teachers make the "adaptations" to activities and materials for individual students. Implementing instructional modifications fall to the special educator or para-educator during the lesson. Little ad hoc lesson modification takes place. Sometimes a general education teacher questions what a special educator is teaching or how he/she is designing instruction for special education students. General education teachers are concerned about the repetition and drill, but the general educators say they have deferred to their colleagues as the "experts".

Special education teachers classify their students in terms of those who could access general education curriculum with no assistance, meaning that they require no special adaptations, and those who needed accommodations. Most of the time, para-educators are assigned to an individual student and spend time either paraphrasing or assisting the student complete his or her own individual tasks. These students have more moderate or severe disabilities and are working on assignments that are only loosely related to what the class is doing. Special education teachers "float" and assist any student that needs help.

In several schools, all students with IEPs, 504 plans, and some other low-achieving students are placed in the same classroom, usually English and math classes at the middle level. Despite the large numbers of students with learning problems, both general and special education teachers believe that this allows them to better target the needs of students and slow down the pace of instruction.

Special education teachers at the upper elementary and junior high school levels express frustration about the performance standards of the state assessments as well as the content that students are expected to learn. Special education teachers feel that the high expectations are good, but the content is irrelevant or unachievable. They believe that they know better what their students need to learn. However, they often confuse the demands for inclusion in general education classes with the state content standards, believing that they can only teach basic or different skills in separate classes or resource rooms.

Bannister School District

The Bannister school district is a large urban district of 175 schools, serving a community of over 700,000. Of the 106,500 students, 86 percent are African-American and 12 percent are white. About 17 percent of the students receive special education and about 70 percent receive free or reduced price meals. One hundred and thirty-three schoolwide Title 1 schools exist in this district.

This urban school district operates in a state that has been implementing a set of standards and a system of performance assessments for over a decade. State standards are linked to a set of performance tests and those results, along with other indicators such as attendance and graduation rates, are reported on school report cards. In addition, for over two decades, the state has had a "minimum competency" graduation test, consisting of four subtests, required by all students for receipt of the high school diploma. Low performing schools can be subjected to sanctions, including state takeovers. Schools that make substantial improvements in student performance can receive cash rewards.

Teachers in this school district are all familiar with the state assessments and of the possible sanctions. The vast majority of schools within the state that have been determined to be eligible for takeover are in this school district. Therefore, teachers are acutely aware of the need to increase student achievement and yet they are not always clear on what it will take to make the types of gains that are required.

Standards and Curriculum

Teachers, both general and special education, say that they teach to the test and that the state assessments influence their instruction more than any other factor. At the middle school, teachers are more concerned about their students passing the high school assessment than necessarily raising scores on the newer state performance assessment. Teachers simply teach to the test and accept that as necessary and good. The state performance assessments have been frustrating for many teachers as they have tried to use the actual performance tasks as lessons, without a thorough understanding of the underlying concepts, knowledge, or skills. When student performances do not increase, some teachers are at a loss of what could be taught that would result in improved scores.

Teachers are neither resentful nor particularly enthusiastic about the assessments. Most teachers support the state standards and their requirements for "higher-level" and "abstract" thinking. They believe these abilities will be necessary for their students to be competitive in the future but all are concerned about the large numbers of students who they believe will not meet the performance standards.

Teachers are concerned that many of their students lack the general language abilities, including basic reading skills and vocabulary, to do well on the tests. Elementary teachers, in particular, would like the state assessments to include some "more basic" items such as traditional reading comprehension questions or math word problems. They feel that their students do poorly because they cannot even understand the task that is required on the assessment.

The district does have a curriculum that is "more or less" aligned with the state standards and assessments and is moving to adopt a standard basal reader and math text. At the middle school, the curriculum is entirely online. Teachers say that they rely on the district curriculum, but most are also dependent on a textbook for guidance with lesson plans and end-of-unit tests for the ongoing assessment of progress.

Instruction and Materials

Teachers say that they "are told what to teach" by the district and/or their principal and most have adopted various instructional programs or interventions, such as an integrated language arts (ILA) program, or a hands-on science program. Most of these programs are "packaged" and come with texts, teacher guides, instructional objectives and strategies, even lesson plans. Teachers are expected to follow the program verbatim.

Instruction is mostly teacher-driven. The standard mode of instruction is for teachers to teach a lesson and then provide a worksheet or other related seat work for individual students to complete. Group work is limited to primary grades and consists of completing individual worksheets related to the lesson. Technology is rarely used in the classrooms and students engage in mostly paper and pencil tasks. Teachers feel that they need a great many more materials to assist them with instruction. Their biggest concern is the lack of motivation and focus among their students. They feel that more interesting materials might help engage students in learning.

Teachers use their own observations of student work to assess progress. All say that they use portfolios and assessments from textbooks. More structured assessments are not often used, and schools vary in terms of how well they analyze the state assessment results and develop school improvement goals.

Students with Disabilities

The state expects most students with disabilities to participate in the state assessments. Thus, special education teachers are aware of the assessment requirements and standards. Special education teachers say that they learn these by looking at what general education teachers are teaching and then "going to a lower level." In many cases, this translates to getting a textbook at a lower grade level and using that as the curriculum. Special education teachers may also supplement the textbook lessons with their own worksheets or activities. This instruction is guided by the IEP goals of students. Since most special education occurs in separate classes, students are grouped by age and functional levels. Teachers interpret access to the curriculum very broadly. Since most of the students have IEP goals that address reading and math, special education teachers say that they are addressing the state standards and that students have access to the general education curriculum.

Special education teachers do not believe that their students can attain the state standards. Some have questioned the relevancy of the standards to students with such low skill levels. Most of the special education students, teachers believe, will likely not graduate and will need vocational skills.

Watertown School District

The Watertown school district is a small, affluent, independent school district with about 5,000 students of whom 94 percent are white, two percent are African-American, and two percent Hispanic. It consists of 12 comprehensive schools. About 12 percent of the students are identified as needing special education and over 1 percent of these come from outside of the district on tuition. About 10 percent of the students in this district receive free and reduced lunch meals.

The district has a long history of supporting public education and exists in a state with a tradition of local control. Test scores of students are among the highest in the state and the district has been recognized in several surveys as the "best" district in the state. About 85 percent of all graduates enroll in full or part-time higher education.

Reform initiatives in Watertown are almost totally locally driven. The district embraced "outcomes-based education" (OBE) and defined nine exit outcomes required for graduation. These are linked to K–12 standards and a system of assessments that include standardized norm-referenced and criterion-referenced tests and portfolios. Much of the emphasis on assessments is at the teacher level. The focus is on helping teachers develop and use assessments to guide instruction, rather than for any high-stakes accountability. The system goals, standards, and indicators were first developed at the high school and have gradually moved downward so that now all teachers are aware of the student requirements. Teachers have been very involved with developing curricular frameworks based on the outcomes and indicators, and there is a general sense of ownership and endorsement of the outcomes.

High school students are required to construct portfolios to demonstrate mastery of the exit outcomes before they can receive a diploma. However, there has been a great deal of support offered to students to insure that graduate.

The state has developed a set of curricular frameworks in content areas that serve as *de facto* standards; thus, state assessment and accountability is just beginning. The state does require, as part of its accreditation process, districts to assess specific aspects of the curriculum using assessments that the district selects.

Standards and Curriculum

The district has a cohesive curriculum aligned with the outcomes, standards, and indicators. Teachers are uniformly aware of the outcomes and their relation to the curriculum. Teachers have been involved in developing performance assessments and developing portfolios that are aligned with the standards, and they feel that they have certain degrees of freedom within the standards. Teachers have been part of the development of the curriculum as well. They also have had an extensive introduction to standards through state efforts in math, science, and early literacy. A number of Watertown's teachers have served on state-level committees that have developed math or science standards and a new early literacy initiative. Teachers also have had an abundance of professional development, specifically related to reading and math instruction, which has incorporated new pedagogical approaches with new content.

Instruction and Materials

Instruction focuses on insuring that content is integrated and there is an extensive use of technology. At the elementary level, teachers tend to use a variety of flexible groupings including a great use of projects and other student-directed activities. Textbooks are used as guides for skill sequences but are supplemented by a variety of other trade books, materials, and software. Resources, including teachers, are used very flexibly and teachers collaborate, team-teach, and appear very supportive of each other.

Students with Disabilities

The district has a long history of supporting special education students and has a very inclusive philosophy. Thus, few students are educated outside of general education classrooms for any period of time. Special and general educators collaborate and team-teach. Also, paraeducators are available in the schools to assist in the instruction of special education students.

The district has strong expectations that students with disabilities will participate in the district curriculum and be held accountable for achieving the outcomes. However, due to the flexibility and small size of the district and the use of portfolio assessments that provide opportunities for students to demonstrate mastery of standards in various ways, students with disabilities rarely "fail". Even students who may participate in community-based programs receive diplomas.

Despite the high level of support, both special and general education teachers are concerned about the high level of intellectual demands in the content they are now teaching. They are also concerned about the amount of concepts and skills they must teach and how this has accelerated the pace of instruction. They see many students with disabilities falling further and further behind; they also see other students who need more and more reteaching or opportunities for practice. At the middle school, a reading class has been established specifically to improve foundational skills (vocabulary and fluency). The math teachers would like to add other classes, below pre-algebra, for students who are struggling in that content area.

General and special educators have structured co-planning time and work very collaboratively. They have had extensive professional developments in this area. They also tend to have a great deal of professional discretion in how to best structure their interactions and instruction. Teachers tend to collaborate around the curriculum as opposed to around the placement of a student. They work very hard to insure that the students with disabilities have access to the curriculum and instruction, using different materials and more intensive instruction as necessary.

What Do the Cases Tell Us about Ensuring Access to the General Curriculum?

As these case histories demonstrate, teachers are struggling with how to interpret "access" to standards and curriculum for every student.

Some Common Dilemmas

One problem faced by many of the teachers is finding the general curriculum. Too often the teachers interpret the daily or weekly lessons as the curriculum and they spend a great deal of time trying to adjust those lessons so that the special education student would fit in and keep pace. Most often these adjustments result in reducing the level of difficulty. With few exceptions, teachers do not have a long-term view of the curricular goals, nor do they have an understanding of the enduring or essential knowledge that they should be teaching.

A related problem is confusing inclusion or participation in general classrooms with access to the curriculum. Separating what is taught from where it is taught was difficult for many teachers. For example, special education teachers generally seem to believe that if a student is to receive instruction in some basic skills or in areas outside of the focus of the general classroom lesson, this should occur in another setting. Some of the schools, such as those in the Bannister school district, maintain very traditional special education programs, with resource and special day classes. Others embrace a more flexible arrangement where students could move from general classes to one-on-one instruction as needed. However, some schools remain focused on inclusion and feel that there is little time to teach other skills.

Another common problem is the notion of selecting the core or enduring concepts or knowledge that should be taught to a student. The need to pull the critical components out of a lesson or unit and devote time to teaching these is not evident in much of the instructional decision-making. Teachers sometimes appear to be almost on a treadmill, adjusting, modifying, reducing, and generally trying to keep the students with disabilities moving forward in a curriculum without a clear set of goals.

When access seems to work, it is because teachers share a knowledge of the general curriculum and have opportunities to discuss what are the most important aspects of the curriculum to teach. Coupled with this is a sense of shared responsibility for insuring all students have access to the same high quality curriculum and instruction. All teachers and other specialists need to have a clear idea of the outcomes associated with the intended curriculum; that is, they must be able to describe what they expect a student to be able to do as a result of instruction in the curriculum.

Still another common problem for teachers is the lack of a clear set of performance expectations coupled with a rather informal and ad hoc assessment process. Teacher knowledge about a student's progress is based on small slices of his/her performance. Test scores or more formal assessments generally are not used to help define the outcomes or to monitor progress. Box 6.1 provides an example of a skilled performance analysis scenario.

The lack of foundational skills among students poses another dilemma for teachers. Teachers are not adept at analyzing the types of learning difficulties students were having. They know that performance is low and that students are struggling; they also know that certain basic literacy skills are lacking. However, they tend to fall into the trap of, "he can't read or compute; therefore, he can't do more complex thinking." Furthermore, teachers are less than adept at assessing student needs in learning processes and strategies. Notwithstanding the need to provide remediation and fill skill gaps, teachers do not see how to work on two fronts at once to create access to knowledge and improve the learning processes themselves.

Some Common Positive Practices

Despite the dilemmas faced by teachers in the case study districts, some positive practices are evident in the case studies.

First, all teachers are becoming more knowledgeable about the general curriculum as well as the content and performance standards that drive that curriculum. In districts where teachers have had opportunities to develop assessments and be part of the reform effort, their curricular knowledge has been greatly enhanced. Although subject matter knowledge has increased, there is also a greater interest in pedagogy, the science

Box 6.1   Skilled Performance Analysis

Here is an example of the kind of teacher performance analysis that needs to be used to ensure access. This example is from a teacher working in Hanley County commenting on a particular student's score on a writing assessment:

"He scored above Level 1. I know this is not the highest level, but he was really struggling with writing. Mrs. Smith (the special educator) and I had worked and worked all year with him on the writing process. We worked on each step and had him practice writing for different purposes. He seemed to be getting it. I have a portfolio of his writing samples. He showed a lot of improvement, but he needed a lot of support, extra time, and so on. Both of us looked at the results of the writing assessment and were kind of disappointed that it wasn't higher, but we know he knows the process and how to write a strong paragraph."

These teachers had a thorough knowledge of the standards and the specific knowledge, skills, and performances expected of students. They knew that both formal and informal assessments and multiple examples of student work are necessary parts of educational analyses.

of how to teach. Both general and special education teachers use a variety of instructional strategies, including more student projects and student-directed learning activities. However promising, too much instruction remains heavily textbook-driven and reliant on worksheets or other teacher-made materials.

Teacher collaboration has also definitely increased as general and special education teachers communicate and discuss content and student achievement. Related to this is the increased flexibility in some schools in how teachers are used and schedules are developed. As schools attempt to increase opportunities for students to receive instruction in the standards, they must look to using resources more efficiently. Flexible regrouping for instruction, reteaching, and reinforcement is only one strategy. The common denominator in all of these arrangements is the core curriculum goals. The examples in Boxes 6.2 and 6.3 illustrate this point.

The vignettes in Boxes 6.2 and 6.3 point to the difficulties in deciding what to teach a student with a disability. The basic dilemma faced by special educators is what leave in and what to leave out. It is a question of competing priorities. In the current climate of reform, when standards and curriculum have resulted in expanded subject matter and more complex skills and knowledge, decisions about where to focus a finite amount of instructional time become even more critical.

Box 6.2   A Lesson about Egypt

In a fifth-grade classroom in Doyle County, the teacher is presenting a lesson on Egypt and the pyramids. In this class of 23 students are four students with IEPs. Among the four students, one is functionally a non-reader, the other three are about two to three years below this level. All have difficulty attending, poor memory, and organization. One student has significant behavior difficulties and is "on and off" medication. Each child is seen separately by the special education teacher about three or four times a week for intensive instruction in reading as well as learning strategies.

Each student has a worksheet of a passage to read followed by questions to be answered. The questions have been modified for the students with IEPs. The lesson addresses several of the state standards in history as well as reading. The teacher leads a lively discussion with the entire class using guided questioning to explain why the pyramids were built and how they related to religious aspects of Egyptian culture. Then students break into four discussion groups to read the passage and answer the questions as a group. The students with IEPs participate in the class instruction, but during independent work both a general education teacher, an aide, and peers support the individual students. Groups are then reformed for direct skill instruction. The students with IEPs and one other student requiring remediation meet as a group with the special education teacher who does a lesson on the questions "who, what, when, and where" pertaining to the pyramids. There is lively discussion about the most important aspects of building the pyramids using the different forms of questions. Students take turns dictating sentences using who, what, when and where and critique one another's sentences.

What's right with this example?

- The teachers share a common vision of the key concepts and knowledge to be addressed in the lesson.

- There is an active sharing of responsibility for the instruction.

What needs improvement in this example?

Students with disabilities are taken out of the discussion when they could profit from the language and ideas that are being expressed. These could later be expanded or paraphrased through guided questions and answers in a small group

Box 6.3   Supporting Primary Students

In an elementary school in Hanley County, two aides (one special education and one Title 1) and a special education teacher move in and out of three classrooms rooms during a morning block of lessons involving math and science. Among the first and second graders are several students with language delays, a student with mental retardation, and a student with autism. The students with disabilities spend almost all of their time in the classrooms. These students sometimes work on very different tasks than their peers and sometimes are given the same assignment as their peers but are intensely supported by the special education aide. The general math instruction involves basic computation and the students construct word problems using blocks and actual objects in class. The special education teachers are focused on maintaining the students in the inclusive setting and providing instruction that is appropriate to the student's developmental level. Sometimes the tasks look alike (they have the same materials) but require very different responses (one student sorts blocks by size or color, while another does basic addition using the blocks). Often the special education teacher provides direct assistance in the task. Peer helpers work with individual students to help solve certain problems using a variety of manipulative materials.

What's right with this example?

- The programs are individualized.

- There is a focus on inclusion.

- There is sufficient support for individual students.

What needs improvement in this example?

- There is no clear link to the general curriculum.

- Each student has his/her own math goals and teachers are not working to create a common core; rather, they are supporting inclusion and participation.

Good special education teachers make those decisions based on a sound knowledge of the subject matter, the demands or expectations of the standards and state and district assessments, each student's level of performance, knowledge of how students learn different types of material, and the conditions that support learning.

Curriculum-Based Collaboration

Some form of curriculum-based collaboration will be critical to ensuring access to the general curriculum for all students. Up to this point, we have not discussed the importance of professional support and establishing a professional community among special and general educators. In our case studies, all teachers spoke of the importance of colleagues in helping them understand the curriculum as well as identify good instructional practices. Teachers need time to plan together, but that planning needs to be centered around the curriculum.

When curriculum-based collaboration occurs, interactions focus primarily on the knowledge contained in the curriculum as well as on specific accommodations and modifications that will support students who have learning problems (Nolet, 1999; Nolet and Tindal, 1996). In the schools we followed, real access occurred when general and special education teachers talked about the curriculum, had a shared understanding of the key ideas and skills associated with the curriculum, and shared an expectation about what was important for each child with a disability to learn. They collaborated around the curriculum and focused on how to maintain the rigor through differentiated instruction. When this did not occur, special education became a remedial "catch-all" where teachers worked to pull students along in the curriculum.

In order to focus instruction, special and general educators must have a shared language and a strong knowledge of subject matter content. Special education teachers provide the differentiation through presenting subject matter in different ways, using different texts or materials, using technology, and setting expectations. They rely on their general education colleagues for the subject matter content and for guidelines on how to teach a subject so that students with different levels of knowledge can learn. The exact content of this key information may differ for each child with a disability, but the skills and knowledge should be expressed in the form of explicit performance of students. What will they be able to do after the instruction? The targets, as we discussed in the last chapter, should be relevant and attainable, but nonetheless should reflect the key elements of the curriculum. Daily instruction is a step toward the larger goal.

This is exactly what we saw in the schools that were successful at ensuring access. The special and general education teachers we observed and interviewed in those schools frequently engaged in conversation and joint planning around the curriculum. This collaboration occurred in blocks of time at key points during the year, such as at the beginning of each semester or grading period as well as before a specific unit of instruction. At these points, general and special educators discussed the critical concepts, skills, and facts that each child was expected to master at the end of a unit or instructional block. Day-to-day collaboration and planning often focused on accommodations or modifications to specific lessons and "progress" checks. These conversations occurred before or after school and on an "as-needed" basis.

A special education teacher in Watertown who supports several fourth- and fifth-grade teachers spoke of "loading up" on planning time at the beginning of each semester so that she truly understood the end-of-semester goals of instruction across the various subject matter areas. For example, they discussed the goals for reading and language arts. One goal was to have the students read literature and write various interpretative and critical essays relating to plot, character development, and interpretations.

The special education teacher asked her colleagues about the four or five most critical concepts and skills each child should gain by the end of the semester or unit. She then designed a range of accommodations and modifications for each of the students she supported. For three students, this meant providing a different book at a lower reading level and reducing demands for the written assignments (such as two paragraphs versus a page or more). For other students, the special education teacher provided more time for reading the text and provided assistance and reinforcement in the analyses and writing, including the use of various writing software. One student had various portions of the story read to her and verbally answered a set of questions about what a character is and about the plot sequencing.

Special education teachers have tendency to design lessons that demand little of the student and focus on rote skills and simple routines. In the mistaken assumption that not pushing a student means lowered frustration and enhanced self-esteem, instruction may follow the general education curriculum and lesson plan, but be a parallel set of "dumbed down" tasks. Special education teachers often believe they need to provide more routines and more basic skills instruction to reduce the curriculum to the lowest common denominator and focus on reducing failure. These simple lessons do not constitute access.

Again, it is critical for teachers to have a deep understanding of the implications of curriculum standards. Teachers who have a clear vision of what students should know and be able to do as a result of having had access to the curriculum are able to find flexible ways to represent information and for students to be engaged in the curriculum. Teachers who are well grounded in content as well as pedagogical knowledge are able to focus instruction on what is important and avoid seductive but irrelevant information.

The Challenge of Creating Access

Teaching is a profession that seems particularly vulnerable to the influence of changing winds. Whenever a new trend blows through, large numbers of us seem to get carried along by the breeze until the weather changes and we are blown off in a new direction. Standards-based school reform is not just a passing breeze. It is a hurricane that has yet to gain full strength. The world is in the midst of a headlong rush toward the creation of a single, global, information-based economy. Knowledge, problem-solving, and thinking will never be less valued than they are right now. Schools will continue to attract an unprecedented amount of public attention and increasingly demand resources because as the value of knowledge grows, so will the importance of the institutions charged with creating that knowledge.

As the demands society makes on schools change, so will the demands that schools effectively meet the needs of all students. Classrooms today include students who have a wider range of skills and backgrounds than at any time in history. The days when general education teachers could reduce the diversity of skills in their classrooms by referring students out to special education are gone. Today all teachers must be skilled at making accommodations. This is no longer something that only special educators do. World-class standards are challenging for all students, not just students who have disabilities. Standards-based school reforms and IDEA-97 challenge all educators to demonstrate that all students can make meaningful progress in the general curriculum. This is a worthwhile challenge. Failure is not an option.

Appendix

RESOURCES FOR FACILITATING ACCESS

This appendix has been included to serve as a resource for further information on IDEA-97, standards-based reforms, curriculum adaptions, educational technologies, and universal design.

Resources for IDEA-97 and Standards-Based Reform

* **McDonnell, McLaughlin, and Morison's** *Educating One and All: Students with Disabilities and Standards-based Reform* **(Washington, DC: National Academy Press, 1997):** This edited volume addresses how to reconcile educational practices and policies that focus on common learning for all students with those designed to individualize education.

* **The Council for Exceptional Children (CEC)** is the largest international professional organization dedicated to improving educational outcomes for individuals with exceptionalities, students with disabilities, and/or

the gifted. CEC advocates for appropriate governmental policies, sets professional standards, provides continual professional development, advocates for newly and historically underserved individuals with exceptionalities, and helps professionals obtain conditions and resources necessary for effective professional practice.
Address: The Council for Exceptional Children
1920 Association Drive
Reston, VA 20191-1589
Toll-free: 1-888-CEC-SPED, Local 703-620-3660
TTY (text only): 703-264-9446, Fax: 703-264-9494
Web site: http://www.cec.sped.org

* **The National Association of State Directors of Special Education, Inc. (NASDSE)** promotes and supports education programs for students with disabilities in the United States and outlying areas. The NASDSE is a not-for-profit corporation established in 1938 and operates for the purpose of providing services to state agencies to facilitate their efforts to maximize educational outcomes for individuals with disabilities.
Address: The National Association of State Directors of Special
      Education, Inc.
1800 Diagonal Road, Suite 320
Alexandria, Virginia 22314
Phone: 703-519-3800, Fax: 703-519-3808, TDD: 703-519-7008
Web site: http://www.nasdse.org/index.htm

* **The National Center on Educational Outcomes (NCEO)** provides national leadership for the participation of students with disabilities and limited English-proficient (LEP) students in national and state assessments, standards-setting efforts, and graduation requirements.
Address: National Center on Educational Outcomes
University of Minnesota
350 Elliott Hall, 75 East River Road
Minneapolis, MN 55455
Phone: 612-626-1530, Fax: 612-624-0879
Web site: http://www.coled.umn.edu/nceo/

Resources for Curriculum Adapations

* **The ERIC/OSEP Mini-Library on curricular adaptations:** This mini-library consists of the three monographs described here:

    * Deborah Simmons and Edward J. Kameenui's *Toward Successful Inclusion of Students with Disabilities: An Overview of Curricular*

Adaptations (1999): The primary focus of this volume is on designing the cognitive supports to instructional materials for students with disabilities in general education classrooms. The fundamental principles of instructional design are summarized, and six principles of effective curriculum design are discussed.

- Jeanne Shay Shumm's *Adapting Reading and Math Materials for the Inclusive Classroom, Volume 2: Kindergarten Through Grade Five* (1999): This volume summarizes relationships between reading and math performance and referrals to special education. This monograph is intended to provide basic tools for organizing classrooms for adaptations, including a sampler of adaptations that have been used successfully in elementary classrooms.

- Keith Lenz and Jeanne Schumaker's *Adapting Language Arts, Social Studies, and Science Materials for the Inclusive Classroom, Volume 3: Grades Six Through Eight* (1999): This book addresses adapting the curriculum in grades six through eight for language arts, social studies, and science. This monograph also provides examples including adapting existing materials and selecting alternate materials.

Ordering Information for the Mini-Library Series can be received from the Council for Exceptional Children at (888) 232-7733 or by fax at (703) 264-9494.

- **Mid-continent Research for Education and Learning (McREL):** This organization, based in Aurora, Colorado, is a private non-profit entity whose purpose is to improve education through applied research and development. McREL provides products and services, primarily for K-12 educators, to promote the best instructional practices in the classroom. Major research areas at McREL include standards, curriculum, and instruction; assessment and accountability; human development, learning, and motivation; organizational and leadership development; mathematics and science; technology; diverse student populations issues; and evaluation and policy studies. Their Web site is at `http://www.mcrel.org/standards`.

- **Center for Effective Collaboration and Practice:** The U.S. Department of Education's Office of Special Education Programs has funded a center to work with other federal agencies to surmount the barriers to collaboration and knowledge use in the multi-disciplinary, multi-stakeholder, and multi-ethnic context in which children with emotional and behavioral problems live and are served. The Center is engaging in a series of strategic activities designed to help SED community members develop a greater capacity to produce, access, and use information, as well as to collaborate.

Address: Center for Effective Collaboration and Practice, American Institutes for Research
1000 Thomas Jefferson St., NW, Suite 400,
Washington, D.C. 20007
Toll Free: 888-457-1551, Local: 202-944-5400
Email: center@air-dc.org, Web site: www.air-dc.org/cecp

Resources for Learning and Technology

* **Donovan, Bransford, and Pellegrino's** *How People Learn: Bridging Research and Practice* **(Washington, DC: National Academy Press, 1999):** This book provides an overview of the most recent research on human learning, with specific references to classroom practices. The book also presents a research agenda for strengthening the link between what we know about learning and what goes on in America's schools.

* **The Research Institute for Assistive and Training Technologies (RIATT):** This professional development program is capable of delivering high-quality training in assistive technology to professionals throughout the world. This economical distance education program is the result of several million dollars in federal, state, and university funding and the work of nationally known content, instructional, and media experts over the past decade. The Web site is at http://www.nasdse.com.

* **The Learning Technology Center (LTC):** This is a research center at Vanderbilt University's Peabody College of Education. The LTC is a group of 70 researchers, designers, and educators who are internationally known for their work on technology in education. Its members' skills and knowledge cover a wide range of areas including education, psychology, computer science, mathematics, chemistry, organizational administration, public policy, and video and multimedia design. The Web site is at http://peabody.vanderbilt.edu/ctrs/ltc. The LTC publishes a daily news source for the latest news in the world of education and technology entitled LTSeek. LTSeek is accessible at http://ltseek.ltc.vanderbilt.edu.

The LTC also supports the K-12 Learning Consortium, a technology-supported project for exploring, disseminating, and sustaining new visions of student learning. The mission of the Learning Consortium is to improve education through collaborations enhanced by technology. The Consortium is working to help a variety of education stakeholders appreciate the importance of learning with understanding (versus memorizing facts and procedures) and to do so in part by focusing attention on classroom-based activities enhanced by the use of frequent assessments for guiding and monitoring learning. The Web site is at http://canvas.ltc.vanderbilt.edu/lc.

Resources for Universal Design

- **Raymond Orkwis and Kathleen McLane's** *A Curriculum Every Student Can Use: Design Principles for Student Access:* This ERIC/OSEP topical brief provides an overview of the rationale and principles of universal design for learning. The publication is framed in the context of IDEA-97 and the need to provide full access to the general education curriculum for students with disabilities. An appendix provides a framework that summarizes the salient principles of universal design in a practical context to help teachers and other interested individuals consider how the tools employed in the classroom can realistically provide broader access to the curriculum for all students. This monograph is available from the ERIC Clearinghouse on Disabilities and Gifted Education and the Council for Exceptional Children (Telephone/TDD: 800-328-0272, fax: 703-620-2521, email: ericec@cec.sped.org).

- The Center for Universal Design is a national research, information, and technical assistance center that evaluates, develops, and promotes universal design in housing, public and commercial facilities, and related products. The Center is housed at the North Carolina State University and can be accessed online at http://www.design.ncsu.edu/cud/index.html.

- The Center for Applied Special Technology (CAST) is a not-for-profit organization whose mission is to expand opportunities for individuals with disabilities through the development and innovative use of technology. ASTC is accessible at http://www.cast.org. The resources available through CAST include universal design for access and for learning at http://www.cast.org/concepts/concepts_udaccess.htm, teaching strategies including adapting curricula at http://www.cast.org/strategies, and teaching tools at http://www.cast.org/tools.

- The Trace Research and Development Center: Trace is a research center at the University of Wisconsin at Madison that focuses on making off-the-shelf technologies and systems like computers, the Internet, and information kiosks more accessible for everyone through the process known as universal design. Their Web site is at http://www.trace.wisc.edu.

REFERENCES

Armbruster, B.B. and T.H. Anderson. "Frames: Structures for informative text." In *The Technology of Text, Vol. 2*, edited by D. H. Jonassen, 90-104 (Englewood Cliffs, NJ: Educational Technology Publications, 1985).

Armstrong, D.G. *Developing and Documenting the Curriculum*. Needham Heights, MA: Allyn & Bacon, 1989.

Atkinson, R.C. and R.M. Shiffrin. "Human memory: A proposed system and its control processes." In *The Psychology of Learning and Motivation: Advances in Research and Theory (Vol. 2)*, edited by K.W. Spence and J.T. Spence, 89-195 (San Diego: Academic Press, 1968).

Barr, R. and R. Dreeben. *How Schools Work*. Chicago, IL: University of Chicago Press, 1983.

Berliner, D.C. "What's all the fuss about instructional time?" In *The Nature of Time in Schools: Theoretical Concepts, Practitioner Perceptions*, edited by M. Ben-Pertz and R. Bromme (New York, NY: Teachers College Press, 1990).

Blank, R.K. and E.M. Pechman. *State Curriculum Frameworks in Mathematics and Science: How Are They Changing Across the States?* Washington D.C.: Council of Chief State School Officers, 1995.

Bloom, B.S., M.D. Engelhart, E.J. Furst, W.H. Hill, and D.R. Krathwohl. *Taxonomy of Educational Objectives: Cognitive Domain.* New York: Longman, 1956.

Bransford, J.D., A.L. Brown, and R.R. Cocking, eds. *How People Learn: Brain, Mind, Experience, and School.* Washington, D.C.: National Academy of Sciences, 1999.

Bransford, J., R. Sherwood, N. Vye, and J. Rieser. "Teaching thinking and problem solving." *American Psychologist, 41*(10), 1986: 1078-1089.

Brown, A.L. "Metacognitive development and reading." In *Theoretical Issues in Reading Comprehension,* edited by R.J. Shiro, B.C. Bruce, and W.F. Brewer, 453-481 (Hillsdale, NJ: Lawrence Erlbaum Associates, 1980).

Case, R. *Intellectual Development, Birth to Adulthood.* San Diego: Academic Press, 1985.

CTB/McGraw-Hill. *The California Achievement Test.* Monterey, CA: CTB/McGraw-Hill, 1985.

Cuban, L. "Curriculum stability and change." In *The Handbook of Research on Curriculum,* edited by P. W. Jackson. New York, NY: Macmillan, 1992.

de Groot, A. E. *Thought and Choice in Chess.* The Hague: Moulton, 1965.

Deno, S. L. "Curriculum-based measurement: The emerging alternative." *Exceptional Children, 52,* 1985: 219-232.

Deshler, D.D., M.M. Warner, J.B. Schumaker, and G.R. Alley. "Learning strategies intervention model: Key components and current status." In *Current Topics in Learning Disabilities (Vol. 1),* edited by J. D. McKinney and L. Feagans, 245-283. Norwood, NJ: Ablex, 1983.

Dimino, J., R. Gersent, D. Carnine, and G. Blake. "Story grammar: An approach for promoting at-risk secondary students' comprehension of literature." *The Elementary School Journal, 91,* 1990: 19-32.

Espin, C.A. and G.R. Tindal. "Curriculum-Based Measurement for Secondary Students." In *Advanced Applications of Curriculum-Based Measurement,* edited by M. Shinn, 214-253. New York: Guildford Press, 1996.

Fredericksen, J.R., and A. Collins. "A system's approach to educational testing." *Educational Researcher, 18*(9), 1989: 27-32.

Freeman, D. and A.C. Porter. "Do textbooks dictate the content of mathematics instruction in elementary classrooms?" *American Educational Research Journal 26*(3), 1989: 403-421.

Fuchc, L.S. "Computer applications to address implementation difficulties associated with curriculum-based measurement." In *Advanced Applications of Curriculum-Based Measurement,* edited by M. Shinn, 89-112. New York: Guildford Press, 1998.

Gagne, R.M., L.J. Briggs, and W.W. Warner. *Principles of Instructional Design, 3rd ed.* New York: Holt, Rinehart, and Winston, 1988.

Gandal, M. "Beyond special education: Toward a quality system for all students." *Harvard Educational Review 57*(4), 1996: 367-390.

Glaser, R. and M.T.H. Chi. "The nature of expertise: Overview." In *The Nature of Expertise,* edited by M.T. H. Chi, R. Glaser, and M.J. Farr, xv-xxviii (Hillsdale, N. J.: Lawrence Erlbaum, 1988).

Hallahan, D.P., J.M. Kauffman, and L.W. Lloyd. *Introduction to Learning Disabilities*. Boston, MA: Allyn & Bacon, 1996.

Harris, K. and S. Graham. *Making the Writing Process Work: Strategies for Composition and Self-Regulation*. Cambridge, MA: Brookline Books, 1996.

Hoover, H.D., A.N. Hieronymus, D.A. Frisbie, and S.A. Dunbar. *Iowa Test of Basic Skills*. Chicago: The Riverside Publishing Company, 1993.

Howell, K, and V.W. Nolet. *Curriculum-Based Evaluation, 3rd ed*. Atlanta, GA: Wadsworth, 2000.

Hudson, P., B. Lignugaris-Kraft, and T. Miller. "Using content enhancements to improve the performance of adolescents with learning disabilities in content classes." *Learning Disabilities Research and Practice* 8(2), 1993: 106-126.

Kameenui, E.J., and D.C. Simmons. *Toward Successful Inclusion of Students with Disabilities: The Architecture of Inclusion*. Reston, VA: Council for Exceptional Children, 1999.

Klinger, J.K. and S. Vaughn. "Students' perceptions of instruction in inclusion classrooms: Implications for students with learning disabilities." *Exceptional Children, 66*(1), 1999: 23-37.

Laurent-Brennan, C. "The international baccalaureate program." *Clearing House* 71(4), 1998: 197-198.

Lenz, K., J.A. Bulgren, and P. Hudson. "Content enhancement: A model for promoting acquisition of content by individuals with learning disabilities." In *Intervention and Research in Learning Disabilities*, edited by T.E. Scruggs and B.L.Y. Wong, 122-165 (New York, NY: Springer-Verlag, 1990).

Mager, R.F. *Preparing Instructional Objectives: A Critical Tool in the Development of Effective Instruction*. Atlanta, GA: Center for Effective Performance, 1997.

Manzo, A.V. "Teaching for creative outcomes: Why we don't, how we all can." *Clearing House, 71*(5), 1998: 287-290.

Marsh, C. and G. Willis. *Curriculum: Alternative Approaches, Ongoing Issues*. Eglewood Cliffs, NJ: Merrill/Prentice Hall, 1995.

McDonnell, L.M., M.J. McLaughlin, and P. Morison. *Educating One and All: Students with Disabilities and Standards-based Reform*. Washington, DC: National Academy Press, 1997.

McGrew, J.D., M.L. Thurlow, and A.N. Spiegel. "An investigation of the exclusion of students with national data collection programs." *Educational Evaluation and Policy Analysis, 15*(3), 1993: 339-352.

McLaughlin, M.J, V.W. Nolet, L.M. Rhim, and K. Henderson. "Achieving better results through access to the general education curriculum: What Does it Mean?" *Teaching Exceptional Children. 31*(3), 1999.

McLaughlin, M.J., K. Henderson, and L.M. Rhim. "Reform for all? General and special education reforms in five local school districts." Paper presented at the American Education Research Association Annual Meeting, Chicago, IL, March 1997.

National Center for Education Statistics. *Trends in Participation in Secondary Vocational Education: 1982-1992*. Washington, D.C.: U.S. Department of Education, 1996.

National Council of Teachers of Mathematics. *Curriculum and Evaluation Standards for School Mathematics.* Reston, VA: National Council of Teachers of Mathematics, 1989.

Nolet, V.W. "Working together in the 21st century high school." In *Teachers Working Together: Enhancing the Performance of Students with Special Needs,* edited by S. Graham, K. Harris, and M. Pressley. Cambridge, MA: Brookline, 1999.

Nolet, V.W. and G.R. Tindal. "Curriculum-based collaboration." In *Strategies for Teaching Exceptional Children in Inclusive Settings,* edited by E.L. Meyen, G.A. Vergason, and R.J. Whelan. Denver, CO: Love Publishing Company, 1996.

Orkwis, R. and K. McLane. *A Curriculum Every Student Can Use: Design Principles for Student Access. ERIC/OSEP Topical Brief.* Reston, VA: Council for Exceptional Children, 1998.

Posner, G.J. and K.A. Strike. "A categorization scheme for principles of sequencing content." *Review of Educational Research 46,* 1976: 665-690.

Rose, D. *Report of the Developer Working Group on Universal Design of Curriculum.* Peabody, MA: Center for Applied Special Technology (CAST), 1998.

Rossi, R. *Profiles of Students with Disabilities as Identified in NELS:88.* (Report No. NCES-97-254). Washington, D.C.: National Center for Education Statistics, (ERIC Document Reproduction Services No. ED 409 663), 1997.

Rusch, F.R. "Identifying special education outcomes: Response to Ysseldyke, Thurlow, and Bruininks." *Remedial and Special Education, 13,* (6), 1992: 31-32.

Schmidt, W.H., C.C. McKnight, and S. Raizen. *A Splintered Vision: An Investigation of U.S. Science and Mathematics Education.* Dordrecht/Boston/London: Kluwer Academic Publishers, 1997.

Schunk, D.H. *Learning Theories: An Educational Perspective, 2nd Ed.* Englewood Cliffs, NJ: Merrill/Prentice Hall, 1999.

Smith, P.L. and T.J. Ragan. *Instructional Design, 2nd Edition.* Columbus, OH: Merrill/Prentice Hall, 1999.

Stodolsky, S. "Is teaching really by the book?" In *The Teacher as Text and the Text as Teacher,* edited by P.W. Jackson. Chicago, IL: National Society for the Study of Education, 1989.

Thorndike, R.M. *Measurement and Evaluation in Psychology and Education (6th ed.)* Upper Saddle River, NJ: Merrill/Prentice Hall, 1997.

Thorndike, E.L. *Educational Psychology: Vol. 2: The Psychology of Learning.* New York: Teachers College Press, 1913.

Thurlow, M.L. *National and State Perspectives on Performance Assessment and Students with Disabilities.* Reston, VA: Council for Exceptional Children, 1994.

Tindal, G.R. and D. Marston. *Classroom-based Assessment: Evaluating Instructional Outcomes.* Columbus, OH: Charles Merrill, 1990.

Torgesen, J.K. "The learning disabled child as an interactive learner: Educational implications." *Topics in Learning and Learning Disabilities, 2,* 1982: 45-52.

U.S. Department of Education. *Nineteenth Annual Report to Congress on the Implementation of the Individuals with Disabilities Act*. Washington, D.C.: U.S. Department of Education, 1997.

Vanderheiden, G. *Universal Design: What It Is and What It Isn't*. Madison, WI: Trace R&D Center, 1996.

Wagner, M., ed. *The Secondary School Programs of Students with Disabilities: A Report from the National Longitudinal Study of Special Education Students*. Menlo Park, CA: SRI International, 1993.

Weinstein, C.E. and R.E. Mayer. "The teaching of learning strategies." In *Handbook of Research on Teaching, 3rd edition,* edited by M.C. Wittrock, 315-327 (New York, NY: Macmillan, 1986).

Williams, R.G. and T.M. Haladyna. "Logical operations for generating intended questions (LOGIQ): A typology for higher order level test items." In *A Technology for Test-item Writing*, edited by G.H. Roid and T.M. Haladyna, 161-186 (New York: Academic Press, 1982).

Wineburg, S. "On the reading of historical texts: Notes on the breach between school and the academy." *American Educational Research Journal, 28,* 1991: 495-519.

INDEX

CORWIN
PRESS

The Corwin Press logo—a raven striding across an open book—represents the happy union of courage and learning. We are a professional-level publisher of books and journals for K-12 educators, and we are committed to creating and providing resources that embody these qualities. Corwin's motto is "Success for All Learners."